BEYOND THE
SPHERE

ENCOUNTERS WITH THE DIVINE

Alfred Stefan Guart

BALBOA.PRESS

A DIVISION OF HAY HOUSE

Balboa Press books may be ordered through booksellers or by contacting:

Balboa Press
A Division of Hay House
1663 Liberty Drive
Bloomington, IN 47403
www.balboapress.com
1 (877) 407-4847

Because of the dynamic nature of the Internet, any web addresses or links contained in this book may have changed since publication and may no longer be valid. The views expressed in this work are solely those of the author and do not necessarily reflect the views of the publisher, and the publisher hereby disclaims any responsibility for them.

The author of this book does not dispense medical advice or prescribe the use of any technique as a form of treatment for physical, emotional, or medical problems without the advice of a physician, either directly or indirectly. The intent of the author is only to offer information of a general nature to help you in your quest for emotional and spiritual well-being. In the event you use any of the information in this book for yourself, which is your constitutional right, the author and the publisher assume no responsibility for your actions.

Bible scripture from New King James Version

Printed in the United States of America.

ISBN: 978-1-9822-4407-1 (sc)
ISBN: 978-1-9822-4409-5 (hc)
ISBN: 978-1-9822-4408-8 (e)

Library of Congress Control Number: 2020904100

Balboa Press rev. date: 07/23/2020

"Men honor what lies within the sphere of their knowledge, but do not realize how dependent they are on what lies beyond it."

Zhuangzi

For my beloved family: Deorajie,
Jiddu, and Almitra
and
In memory of my faithful mother, Stephanie

CONTENTS

INTRODUCTION

Direct encounters with the Creator have had a profound impact on humanity. The beliefs and values of billions of people can be traced back to some form of Divine Visitation. These contacts taught us who God is, who we are and how we should relate to our Maker and to one another. In order to evolve, existing beliefs must be re-evaluated from time to time. In that spirit, we will take a critical look at historical Visitations, but not before we do something unorthodox: delve into encounters with God I have concealed in my heart and mind for the past forty years.

The reasons for this long silence are many. There is the immensity of direct contact with the Architect of Life, which is overwhelming and transformative. Long reflection is required to process major life experiences. Think about it. How much time would it take to fully grasp receiving $1 billion from a stranger who vanishes? How simply and quickly can we grasp the meaning of a child's birth or the sudden loss of a loved one? Meeting God is no less a life-transforming event.

Not a day has gone by when I haven't tried to make sense of it, to work it into my little life, to figure out why and how it happened. Every day I long for another Divine spiritual embrace and pray for everyone to experience it.

I've also been silent because I expected skeptics, atheists, self-aggrandizing intellectuals and even some religious adherents to mock or denounce what I would have hastily reported. But it's time, four decades is enough to ruminate on these encounters. I approach this task with the same journalistic skepticism I would apply to any hard news story. The reader may also find the Socratic maxim, "The unexamined life is not worth living" animating each chapter. Everything presented here is true and accurate to the best of my ability. Where possible, I've interviewed people who were part of this journey for additional clarity and verification.

For any failures or material omissions, I apologize in advance.

Like one of my spiritual mentors, J. Krishnamurti, I have no interest in cultivating acolytes nor establishing any doctrines or institutions. I write simply as a friend, someone willing to listen and search together for meaning.

In one sense, this book is a personal affirmation that God is real - more alive than anyone or anything I've encountered. Until 1980, I was a committed agnostic and would never have changed without direct experience. There is a difference between *belief* in the Supreme, or advancing a quasi-scientific theory about the necessity of one, and a direct encounter. The latter results in a matter-of-fact acknowledgement that a Reality or Consciousness exists beyond our own. Awareness of that Reality is proof enough. No one is asked to prove their mother existed, right? It is fact. There's no need to believe it, debate it or justify it with a clever argument. Perhaps this is the reason the Creator is simply referred to as *I Am* in Biblical scripture.

This is not an attempt to convince anyone to accept my findings. Rather, I encourage everyone who is interested to find out for themselves. There's no substitution for a serious and thorough investigation of our own.

You will not find within these pages a philosophical treatise for or against the existence of God. As a philosophy student, I followed arguments on both sides of this topic and found reason and logic ineffective. Pro-God philosophers such as Emmanuel Kant, reasoned out their belief in a Creator. For example, one can infer that since nature has laws and evidences design, there must be a law maker/designer. But other thinkers countered there is chaos and war in the world. What God would put cruelty in the *Great Plan*? The answer was to claim God endowed humans with free will. But the free will argument presumes God's existence.

One theory, *Deus Ex Machina* or "God outside the machine" attempted to escape the circular debate by asserting the Almighty created the universe - then backed away to let it run itself. No argument for the existence of a Prime Mover escaped materialists, such as the atheist, Karl Marx. The anti-God thinkers claim we can only rely on what the five senses process. Since no one can prove they have seen, touched, smelled, heard or tasted God, the whole thing is fantasy, a mere academic exercise. It's a philosopher's merry-go-round, and I'm not getting on.

Why not? Because reason itself, while an amazing tool we employ to survive, evolve and prosper on Earth, has its limits. It relies on existing thought, accepted facts and experience. It has strict rules. How can we use something so limited to understand something infinite? You don't peer into a microscope to see the constellations. You can't experience the full diversity of oceanic life from a single drop of salt water. Reason insists the Omnipresent squeeze into a tiny box so we can see it, hold it, prove it is real. You cannot reason your way to God. This leaves two paths for exploring Divinity: direct encounters and indirect experiences of faith.

Encounters with the Almighty have been reported since the beginning of recorded history. Eastern mystics, Biblical prophets and saints left a record of so-called religious experiences. These events are part of human history, however underreported and misunderstood. How frequent or how rare they are, I do not know. How reliable? Are they the product of imagination, mental illness, drugs? Do they matter? One thing is clear. Reports from those who have described encounters with God are fairly consistent: there's something unfathomable *out there*.

Reports of God visits have been varied and sometimes contradictory. God has been described as petty yet mysterious, as murderous yet unconditionally loving, as requiring a code of conduct or not, as wanting blood sacrifices or not, and as having a personality or not. These renditions of life's Source have impacted billions of minds, sometimes in harmful ways. For this reason alone, reports of Divine Visitation deserve our attention.

Faith is another way to engage the great I Am and is what most religions advocate. In faith we are asked to accept God as a given - without direct encounter. We build a relationship with the Almighty, albeit an indirect one. We are encouraged to pray, attend church, synagogue or mosque, to sacrifice and tithe. Often someone in the religious hierarchy intercedes with the Deity on our behalf. Most religions set out a code of conduct so we may avoid offending God and reinforcing our alienation.

In faith, we hope to see evidence of God working in our lives, answering prayers and uplifting us. When we don't see prayers answered, preachers provide various explanations and cite scriptures. They earnestly work to give us hope. Oddly, religion, which etymologically means to *re-bind* us to our Source, accepts alienation from God as the norm. We don't expect communion with the Deity, at least not on Earth. And in some religious circles, claiming an encounter with God could be met with harsh accusations of blasphemy. We are led to lower our expectations and dream of meeting our Maker only after we die.

So, putting philosophy and theology aside, we examine religious experience with an organic approach. From the spiritual soil and seed to the plant and, ultimately, the flower. This book begins by providing pertinent personal and familial background and explores key events that culminate in the ecstatic encounters. Father Time has provided a way to see early life experiences as precursors, hints of what was to come. One can almost feel the outstretched arm of God reaching through the clouds of my ignorance, immaturity and self-interest, getting closer and closer until that first momentous contact. God, the omniscient stalker.

With the background set, I will convey - with the limitation of words - two direct encounters with the Infinite that altered the course of my life. Though some details are long forgotten, the places and circumstances of these visitations remain vivid. Interestingly, the first visitation overflowed with sheer jubilance. The second, also imbued with joy, left me weeping as never before.

We will also briefly examine the lives of those who allege to have had contact with Heaven. Did these people have anything in common that could have made them particularly vulnerable to spiritual encounters?

The remaining chapters center on the struggle to integrate the Visitations into a normal life of earning a living and raising a family in, of all places, New York City. Given that reality, some questions emerge: Does the Creator play a role in our professional, financial and emotional well being? Can a life of faith be offered as proof religious encounters are real? Are we pursuing God or is it the reverse? Finally, why do so few people report having communed with God?

Our explorations lead us to discuss possible causes of and solutions to the condition of spiritual alienation. What can we do to step outside the insulating spheres we sustain by our self-absorption? To what extent can we lift the veil and touch upon a new and different world? How do we raise our children to be sensitive to all living things, thus giving them a greater chance of encountering the fullness of life, of experiencing Presence?

Interspersed in these chapters you will also find ideas and references to spiritual and philosophical mentors. These were the fathers who filled the emptiness left by the absence of my own biological father. Among them: Jiddu Krishnamurti, Jesus, Khalil Gibran, Lao Tzu, Gautama Buddha and Biblical prophets.

Finally, a word about terms you will encounter. To avoid repetition, *God* is referred to alternatively as Presence, Deity, Yahweh, G-d, Source, Truth, Great Spirit, Architect of Life and other phrases. By *sphere*, I mean the invisible boundary between ourselves and the rest of the world, as well as the psychological contents gathered within that intangible barrier. I do not mean a physical, perfect orb.

I pray this endeavor will result in more souls having their own direct encounters with the Divine and encourage everyone to seek Truth for themselves.

CHAPTER ONE

SPIRITUAL ROOTS

"I had no idea what it was. I felt this pressure and I couldn't get up, I couldn't scream, I couldn't talk, I couldn't do anything."

Jessica Alba

I t was the Summer of 1980 when God exploded into my life. I was a fatherless twenty-two year old, an outsider drawn to philosophers, spirituality, martial arts and natural foods. Several mornings each week my roommate, Joe Piegari, and I rode the subway at 5 a.m. from Park Slope, Brooklyn to a Manhattan school run by legendary Kung Fu master Alan Lee. The workouts were tough and it was common for students to vomit during the warm-up. We enjoyed the physical challenge and the confidence of knowing we could disable a would-be attacker of any size or strength with a quick strike. We thought we were hot stuff being able to do pushups on our thumbs and perform devastating flying side kicks. As time passed my interest turned toward the mystical underpinnings of Kung Fu: Taoism. That, I sadly learned, was not the focus of the school.

Taoism and all non-Christian religions interested this rebellious Catholic. Yes, I was baptized and completed the rites of Holy Communion and Confirmation. My family celebrated all the holidays - Good Friday, Easter, Christmas. And I was never molested. But I was an inquisitive boy and by the time I reached twelve, the church seemed to run out of answers to satiate my thirsty mind.

The break with Catholicism came at a Midnight Mass on Thirteenth Street off Fourth Avenue in Brooklyn, once dubbed the *Borough of Churches and Baby Carriages*. It was a cold night. A light snow fell as my mother and I walked the four city blocks to the church. When we got there, I held the door open and said, "I'm gonna wait for you out here, ma." Disappointed, my mother went in. I just couldn't keep sitting in a pew, standing and kneeling on command and repeating the well worn chants, songs and prayers. The memory of my last church visit didn't help. I had watched a cockroach zig zag along the collar of a tattered wool coat worn by an old lady in the pew ahead of us. This went on for nearly the entire mass. I stood outside the church as long as I could, but the cold got inside my coat. So I stepped into the vestibule, hoping no adults would come in or out and question my boycott. It was awkward loitering there between the freezing night air and the comfort of the Twelve Stations of the Cross.

Although Catholicism was losing one more lay member, spirituality remained a stubborn yet puzzling part of my young life. Raised solely by my mother's side of the family - those of Spanish and Puerto Rican descent - I witnessed many seances. My mother, aunts and one great aunt would gather around a table ("mesa" in Spanish) featuring a glass of water and a candle. Holding hands in the darkness, they chanted and prayed in Spanish with increasing intensity until one of them would moan and fall into a trance.

My sisters, cousins and I would watch in stunned silence as the event's chosen medium would go limp, as if her spirit had left her body. Sometimes it was my great aunt, Montserrat, who we called Tia Montse, but other times it was my Aunt Jenny. Everyone else at the mesa would remain silent. Then the medium would stiffen back up, her body presumably inhabited by another spirit. It was normal to hear from dead relatives who would sometimes identify themselves - or be asked to. Her eyes would open and she'd begin peering into the glass of water and passing her hands over it.

Soon she would reveal the events being shown to her in the glass of water, which was illuminated only by the candle. Visions only she could see would explain conditions in the spirit world wreaking havoc on our lives. Next, each participant took turns asking questions about their own struggles. Each would be offered steps they could take to address their concerns, usually some kind of ritual like burying a piece of clothing or setting up a shrine. Since all this was in Spanish, and kids were raised to speak only English, we had no idea what was being revealed. Though we saw nothing in the candlelit water glass, it all seemed important to our elders.

For a kid, seances can be frightening and confusing. The grandame of these gatherings was Tia Montse. Like my grandmother, she was a brown-skinned Taino born in Puerto Rico who never learned English. She kept herself fit in her old age and I recall her demonstrating how she could still bend to place her palms flat on the floor. My grandmother also had the gift of spiritual abilities, but my mother did not. At least one of my aunts would occasionally serve as a messenger from the *other side*. Apparently, this matriarchal mediumship dated back centuries. My earliest recollections of these seances have me standing tiptoed to see over the edge of a table, only to be shooed away.

The mesas were not some kind of money-making storefront scam. Mesas were only held for family during hardships as a means of getting spiritual guidance from the departed. On rare occasions, a relative would bring a trusted friend in need of assistance. Obviously, there are those who claim to be mediums or psychics who are outright frauds and who prey on the vulnerable for their money. There was none of that in my family. These were true believers. One might question their motives and guidance, but there never was a scheme to defraud anyone of cash. I included these events to shed light on the spiritual aura of my childhood and to introduce Tia Montse, who would reappear just months before my encounters with the Almighty.

As a boy, I was subject to several psychic or spiritual events outside of the mesas. One could argue these episodes were due to a medical condition, simply imagined or a product of psychological conditioning. I take no position on whether spiritual experiences are evidence of an afterlife or the result of sleep deprivation, chemical imbalance, or anything else. I merely present the experiences faithfully to provide context for what comes later.

One type of psychic event involved waking up in bed paralyzed, or what scientists today call *sleep paralysis*. In this state, I could see and hear everything but was unable to move any part of my body other than my eyes. During these terrifying moments, I helplessly saw and heard strange things. Once it was an apparition that looked like a demented clown who screeched "Catch me if you can" as it raced by my bed and leaped out a window. I felt glad it didn't stick around for a chat. Another time, when I was in my twenties, I awoke to sinister, whispered laughter coming from a group of miscreants gathered by my bedroom door. The door was to my right, but I couldn't turn my head to see them. As is common during these episodes, there was that sense of being vulnerable in the face of danger. My mother advised me when I was young to make the sign of the cross at those moments and many times I struggled to but was usually unable to do so. Another solution was to wear a crucifix and reach for it or keep a Bible under your pillow.

These rude awakenings began in my preschool days and continued well into my forties. A potentially lucrative one took place in the early 2000s as I slept in my Kensington, Brooklyn home. I was a reporter for the *New York Post* at the time and needed a good night's rest for that highly competitive job. This night I awoke to footsteps entering the bedroom, but it was dark and I saw no one. A voice whispered "Freddy," a nickname only family and boyhood friends would know. The voice that was coming from near the foot of my bed sounded like my recently deceased sister, Stephanie. I indignantly struggled to see who had violated the sanctity of my home and sleep, but remained immobile. I demanded the intruder show themselves and threatened to rise out of bed and make them regret waking me. "Freddy," it whispered again.

"I'll give you to three to tell me who you are," I demanded. "One, two, three!"

At that I managed to sit up in bed, fully awake and frustrated, with my eyes open. The only thing visible was the alarm clock, which beamed "1:23" in glowing red letters. The numbers I had just called out as an ultimatum were now the only things I could see in that darkened room. Later that day

I shared the incident with my mother thinking she might take comfort in her daughter's possible visitation. "You've got to play that number," she said, catching me by surprise. I'm no gambler, but saw no harm in plunking a few dollars down on a lottery ticket. To my surprise, I ended up a few hundred dollars richer that day. So did my mother. Wish I had wagered more.

There were other episodes of sleep paralysis, but the last occurred around 2005. I was forty seven. My eyes opened to an unfamiliar bedroom ceiling, then an open doorway that led to a hall and a flight of stairs. A skylight bathed a bannister, pink walls and cranberry red carpeting in filtered sunshine. My mind was vulnerable, quiet, soaking in the new environment. Everything I laid eyes on was fresh and exciting. Surveying the strange surroundings led to the startling revelation that all memory had been erased. I had awakened to a state of amnesia, a stranger in a strange land. Without memory, there was no *I* or *me* or *mine*. What was seen was not my bedroom ceiling, although I had painstakingly installed every tongue and groove pine board and every recessed lighting fixture. The bannister didn't belong to me, although I had painted every baluster white myself. All personal memory was wiped clean just as it would have been for a computer hard drive.

The absence of all memory and identity briefly created a spark of panic. However, it vanished as simple curiosity allowed the moment to flower. "Shhh. Let's check this out." It was as if I had intruded onto something secret, taboo and special. It was energizing to see the world afresh, not shrouded by the past. My mind was light, not weighed down by experience - a leaf floating on the wind. But soon memory crept back, so subtly, like a thin veil slowly covering the freshness of that moment. I could feel the memory data refilling my mind until *I* was back in *my* bed, sitting up and looking at *my* familiar bedroom ceiling and *my* hallway with the illumination coming from *my* skylight.

Sleep paralysis has been documented across the globe for centuries, usually with a supernatural explanation. Prophets such as Ezekiel and Daniel, early Christians like Paul, and the founder of Islam, Muhammad, all claimed to have received visions and spiritual visits while in bed at night. Some claim to have seen demons during terrifying episodes. Gautama Buddha is said to have gained control over this phenomenon. Some researchers suggest sleep paralysis, as well as related out of body experience, are common threads linking the founders of every religion.

Sufferers of sleep paralysis may encounter sexualized spirits, such as Incubus. More common is a murderous demon pressing on their chests, trying to prevent them from breathing. Indeed, the word *nightmare* comes from sleep paralysis encounters in Europe where it was common for sleepers to awake to find a phantom horse standing or riding on their chests.

Recently, scientists have delved into the matter and found sleep paralysis takes place when we wake during REM sleep. During the Rapid Eye Movement stage, sleepers dream and are prevented from physically acting out their fantasies by chemicals released into the body which limit movement. Scientists also are inclined to believe demons, horses, witches and all other entities are hallucinations that would normally be part of a dream. Only about eight percent of the world's population experience sleep paralysis, and it usually starts in the teen years. The research, while seeming to dismiss the supernatural, is neither exhaustive nor conclusive. For my part, I report the experiences without judgment other than to suggest the state of awareness that sometimes takes place during sleep paralysis - where memory is absent and consciousness is in a state of innocence - is what many spiritual masters described as the goal of meditation. Zen acolytes refer to it as the *beginner's mind*.

In my youth, premonitions also took place, but were sporadic and limited to life and death matters. Like the time my grandmother walked my sister and I towards home after a visit. Grandma had remained in her apartment in a six story walk-up on Nelson Street after we moved to a private house on Fourteenth Street and Second Avenue in the shadow of the Brooklyn Queens Expressway. The three of us reached the Hamilton Avenue drawbridge over the Gowanus Canal to part company and my sister and I took turns kissing grandma. The moment I kissed grandma's cheek I knew it was the last time I'd see her. I was about 10 years old. Not long after that kiss, grandma went missing and it caused a stir in our home. I recall my mother and aunts engaged in whispered conversations before they left our house. They returned hours later, having identified grandma's body at the morgue. She had been hit by a yellow taxi that was racing toward the entrance of the Brooklyn Battery Tunnel.

Roughly five years later, my grandfather, Gerardo Guart, was hospitalized. A Catalan who immigrated from Spain and a lifelong smoker, he was undergoing tests for a lung ailment. In the middle of one Summer's night, the house phone rang. I awoke on the first ring and the words "Grandpa's dead" came to mind. The phone rang again. I heard my mother's voice answering. Suddenly, I heard wailing. We all got up and went to her room. Grandpa's lungs had filled with blood during the night and he'd died by the time hospital staff discovered it.

Spirituality often expressed itself as connectivity. In my early twenties, I would sometimes know when people close to me were troubled. For example, once while taking a shower the tile walls seemed to suddenly close in on me, coming within inches of my face. I lost depth perception and balance for a moment. Just as quickly, it stopped. That evening I described the strange episode to my Kung Fu partner, Joe. He asked me what time it happened and was shocked at my answer: At that moment he was experiencing his first hypoglycemic event with the same symptoms.

A few times groups of seagulls flying overhead in the area between the Green-Wood Cemetery and Prospect Park seemed to convey messages or impressions. I recall once feeling a friend was in danger. I contacted them to see if they were okay and learned they had been in a car accident. The invisible bonds between humans have been with us for centuries. But can these connections serve as conduits for communication? Such as when someone pops into your consciousness that you haven't heard from for a while and you run into them or they call. In a handful of instances, people in my personal circle have reported my appearance in dreams. Usually there is a message conveyed. In one extreme example, someone reported seeing me smiling and waving at them while in a park on two occasions. The park was in Washington, D.C. I was in New York.

From my earliest memories, I could never walk directly behind anyone. Friend or foe, family or stranger, I followed no one. Crowded street or not, I had to move to the left or right. Sometimes it was hard to find a lane of my own, but I always did. This may be related to not knowing my father. But it may also have influenced my search for a direct encounter with Truth.

Finally, I'm not sure how this is relevant, but it may be. I recall a recurring black and white dream I had throughout my elementary school years. In it are two objects: a black vertical line and a transparent, nearly weightless sphere. Both are seen against a white background. The sphere is in constant, random motion and the line is beneath it, struggling to maintain contact. The line's purpose is to keep the sphere from dropping because then all motion would cease. It's like an animated, geometric dance.

And I was the line. Let the shrinks have at it.

CHAPTER TWO

THE PRESENCE

"A father of the fatherless, a defender of widows, is God in His holy habitation,"
Psalms 68:5 (NKJV)

I n my late teens, a co-worker introduced me to the teachings of Indian mystic and philosopher Jiddu Krishnamurti. I read his books with keen interest, the first being *Think on These Things*. His call for people to put aside all ideologies and religious doctrines in order to seek Truth for themselves resonated. Some might say that resonance resulted from lacking a father figure and a general discomfort with authority.

Amazed at the intelligence and liberating insight of Krishnamurti, I shared *Think on These Things* with my small circle of friends and we began having long discussions. A group of us once went to a Manhattan bookstore where a videotape of one of K's speeches was shown. (Krishnamurti was known as "K" or "Krishnaji" to many of his associates).

One evening Joe Piegari and I delved so deeply into K's teachings on the limitation of thought we reached a point of wordless, inward silence. We had stumbled into an area where ideas and words were simply distractions or hindrances. We unwittingly entered into that vital realm beyond self. As we sat pleasantly surprised by the pregnant silence, a spiritual presence occupied the room. It was simply there, unobtrusive, yet encompassing us and everything else. Someone spoke and it dissipated. We compared notes afterward to ensure it had really happened.

The presence showed up again about a year later. A girlfriend and I were sitting at the kitchen table one evening in a basement apartment I shared with Joe P. Joann and I both worked at Paragon Sporting Goods on Broadway in Manhattan. She was a true Bohemian who lived for the day. Tall and blonde with sky blue eyes and the face of a cherub. We often talked about K's insight and shared any kernels of spiritual truth we found. As we talked at the table, we felt the presence enter the room. It seemed to be behind and just above me. I didn't look back. It felt as though it was letting us know there were plans in place that would require my leaving. I took her hands in mine and said, "Wherever it takes me, I will take you."

Being so influenced by K, I could never accept the truth of another. I refused to be what he dubbed a "second-hand person." If God existed, if there was a purpose to life, I would have to find out myself. Directly. No doctrines, no interpreters, no interceders. I also took seriously his call to remove fear and took drastic steps to do so. Fear, K taught, creates psychological limitations that form a barrier between us and reality or Truth.

To overcome fear and find the Truth, I once walked seven blocks to Prospect Park in the throes of a thunderstorm. When there, I wrapped my arms around a tree.

On another night, I walked to the park and lay down in an open field close to the baseball diamonds. The sky was clear, and being in the park allowed stars to be visible. I looked at the twinkling lights, but was unmoved. I wanted to feel something from looking at the infinite sky, yet came up empty. I desperately needed to know whether there was a purpose to life. Was there more to life for us than to work, procreate and die? It seemed so empty and nihilistic.

Alone in that starlit field I begged God, if there was one, to answer me. Otherwise, I didn't see the point of it all. I closed my eyes as tears trickled down my cheeks and into my ears. "Please show me a sign," I pleaded. I opened my eyes and looked up to the night sky for a sign. A shooting star streaked by, and, for a moment there was a sense of wonder. I got off the ground and wiped my eyes, unsure whether the fleeting meteorite was a sign or a mere coincidence.

I'd like to point out, simply going to Prospect Park alone at night in the 1970s was putting your life at risk. For instance, killings in New York City hit a record breaking 1,700 in 1979. Crime was so rampant, Joe P. and I used to test how callous people had grown. We'd stand on the side of the road that wound through the park, roughly 100 yards from a stoplight. When cars stopped for the light, one of us would push the other across the road with the headlights of the stopped cars shining on us. We knew we were seen.

Reaching the other side, the "mugger" who had shoved his "victim" across the road would raise his arm and pretend to stab his hapless victim (with a comb). This grisly scene would end with the victim "dying" on the ground and the startled mugger deliberately stopping to look at the oncoming cars before disappearing into the night. No one ever stopped to help. We would hold our sides with laughter.

Well, there was one time a car did stop. "Hey, you alright," I could hear someone from the backseat of the stopped vehicle yell as I fled the scene. I turned back, only to see Joe P. sit up as a man got out from the rear door of the sedan to help. Joe scrambled towards me, yelling "Cops!"

The undercover police chased us through open fields, up and down hills in their unmarked car. We took refuge in a muddy briar patch, keeping still and silent until they left the area. Then we laughed, relieved we had dodged a bullet - but not without scratches and itches.

This was also a time I learned there was healing power in my hands. People close to me would come for help with health conditions. Once my roommate woke in severe pain. He came to my room groaning and holding his lower back. I placed my hands on the area and in a few minutes the pain vanished. He drove to the hospital, where he learned he had a kidney stone. I also relieved headaches for others. My own headaches? Nothing I could do.

I enjoyed Prospect Park as it was as close to nature as I could get in Brooklyn. I taught martial arts there to local kids and helped my friend, Bobby Brown, coach a softball team. As per K, I took no drugs. Not even aspirin. I drank distilled water. So, when I fell and sliced my thumb open on a piece of glass while playing frisbee with my ragtag martial arts students, we walked to the Methodist hospital emergency room.

On the way, I could see bone through the cut. The doctor said it would have to be stitched. I refused anesthesia. The doctor tried several times to convince me to dull the pain. But I held firm. With every stitch, I kept my left hand still, breathing in and out while transferring all tension to my right arm. When it was over, my young students greeted me in the waiting room and we walked out together. Also during this period, I had a filling replaced without anesthesia.

The stitched thumb proved to be the beginning of a stressful time. I found myself getting hurt frequently and inexplicably. It seemed I was bleeding almost daily from one extremity or another. One night my bike hit a pothole, sending me head-first into a lamppost. A glass I was washing dropped and shattered, cutting my hand. For several days this went on. There was an ominous aura stalking me that I couldn't shake.

The following is an instance from that time I had completely forgotten. Joe P. reminded me of it and I asked him to put it in writing. He refers to me as "Freddy," a nickname my family came up with as "Alfred" seemed too formal to them. Joe in his own words:

"We stood on the upper floor of my parent's home, which formerly had served as my grandparent's apartment, between the living room and the kitchen where Freddy had simply froze, which had caused me to stop.

"What is it now?" is all I could think to myself. We'd been walking toward the kitchen door and had planned to head outside. A look of introspection now held him in place.

"Would you stand here?" he said to me.

"No." That had become my first reaction to everything he asked of me. Nothing was simple with this guy.

"Come on. Just stand here."

"Why?"

"Because I want you to feel something."

"You want me to feel something?"

"Yes."

"And if I stand there, I'm going to feel it?"

"I don't know."

"Do you have any idea how creepy that sounds?"

I couldn't help but think that while I'd grown close to Freddy in the short while we'd known each other, I'd also grown wary of this other side of him, these 'spiritual' experiences which I wanted no part of.

Whether manifestations of the same thing or not, he often had an uncommon perspective on situations, on life. Where I saw nothing, he saw great sadness – until he pointed it out to me; where I only felt fear, he saw injustice which needed to be righted. He'd once convinced me to walk a black guitar player, whom we'd discovered cowering in a phone booth, past "our friends." We quickly discovered that they'd beaten him up for being black, and Freddy insisted we take him to the local train station and wait with the musician until he'd boarded his train. All I'd seen was some guy who looked both afraid and angry – someone who had his own problems, which I'd wanted no part of.

"Don't worry." he'd said to the musician. "Nobody is going to hurt you."

"Yeah." I said, not so sure as there were eight of "our friends" and only two of us. And they didn't like what we were doing.

So while the request to simply stand in a spot might seem whimsical, where Freddy was involved,

I already understood that I really had no idea what I might be getting myself into.

I approached the spot cautiously.

"There," I said. "So what am I supposed to be feeling?"

"Come on. You're not even in the spot."

I edged closer, and out of frustration he muscled me into this place just as he stepped out of it. Instantly, I felt incredibly cold, but I had no intention of telling him that. Skeptical by nature and more so in the presence of my close friend whom I suspected of being a bit unhinged, I refused to disclose anything. For it to be real, he would have to confirm first what I already felt.

"So?" I asked.

"Don't you feel that?"

"Feel what?"

"The intense cold?"

"Yeah. So what's that supposed to mean?"

He wouldn't tell me.

"Step away from the spot." I did. "What do you feel now?"

"It's warmer."

"Now step back."

I did.

"Okay. So there's a cold spot just outside the kitchen. What does that prove?"

"Where there are no drafts."

"Okay."

"No windows nearby."

"Yes. So what? What does it mean?"

"Well," he said matter of factly, "there's a spirit standing there."

I felt sick inside.

"What?"

"A spirit."

"You mean like a ghost?"

"You know... a lost soul."

I stepped out of the spot.

"So why do you have me step into this place where some lost soul is standing? What is wrong with you? Couldn't you leave the poor thing alone? Why did you have to have me go and bother it?"

He was laughing now.

"I wanted to know if you felt it too."

"Well I did. And I could have done without that. Can we go now?"

As we walked down the stairs, I thought about all the times my mother had spoken about my grandparent's apartment being haunted, about how she'd tried to get a priest to perform an exorcism of the entire house, but had to settle for having the house blessed instead."

Shortly after that incident, the creepiness came to a head one night while I was alone in the apartment. A malevolent presence took residence, one more bold and threatening, not just a creepy, cold spot in the room. I moved cautiously through the apartment, fearing something in it would cause serious injury. I was afraid to go outside fearing a car accident, a violent mugging or other fatal events awaited. There I was, a normally fearless person, paralyzed with dread.

Out of worldly options, I telephoned my mother and explained what was happening, knowing she wouldn't dismiss it out of hand. She told me it just so happened Tia Montse was on her way over and invited me to join them. It was only a half mile walk to mom's. I'd done it many times. But not this time.

"Your sister's here," my mom said. "She'll drive over and pick you up."

I reluctantly agreed and remained tense the entire car ride. Once at my mother's, Tia Montse, who almost never visited mom's, was seated at the kitchen table opposite my mother. After some small talk, I sat next to my mom. Tia Montse went to work ... I mean into a trance. Soon she was speaking Spanish and my mother was translating. It was my first and only time as a participant in a "mesa." Her pronouncements were unexpected and disturbing.

The first thing she said was that the bleeding incidents had been inflicted by a *cura* (pronounced coo dah) or priest. This priest was with me since birth, but incensed I never joined the priesthood. For this betrayal he wanted me dead. Tia Montse went on to reveal two protective spirit guides were standing beside me. One was a very "intelligent" and "wise" Jew named Samuel. The other she described as a very powerful spirit she called "El Indio" or the Indian.

I was skeptical, of course. First, her explanation sounded ridiculous, like the opening line of a barroom joke or the plot to a soap opera we could call *Days of Our Spirit Lives*. Even if true, Tia Montse's assertions would be dubious to anyone who'd grown up on the streets of Brooklyn. I wanted to interrupt and ask why the two good spirits, one being so smart and the other so powerful, couldn't team up and neutralize the hell-bent priest so we could put this whole thing to bed.

But I was in no position to argue with Tia Montse. She was still in a trance and only trying to help. Besides, seance's weren't *60 Minutes* interviews. You got what you got and allowed for the chance finer details could be lost in translation. And who knew? Perhaps the rules of the street didn't apply to the spiritual path. So my takeaway was a bloodthirsty priest wanted me dead, while Samuel and El Indio were guiding and protecting me. What, I wondered, was I supposed to do with that?

Tia Montse's prescription was I go home and keep a candle lit for seven days so Samuel could help me. Candles provide light and energy the spirits need, she said. Then she motioned for me to stand. She passed her hands over my head and down the sides to my feet and back up three times without making physical contact. As she did, I closed my eyes. I felt elated, relieved, liberated. For a moment I saw myself in wind-blown robes, standing among clouds in the night sky.

"She said something very great is going to happen in your life soon," my mother said. I went home optimistic. Next day, I bought a large candle for Samuel and prayed he would have the strength to guide me. I was still an agnostic. However, I couldn't argue with success. The bleeding stopped and the psycho cura was gone.

One thing kept bothering me, though. Tia Montse's pronouncement about a killer priest stirred long abandoned memories. As a preschooler, I would sneak into the bathroom of our railroad apartment on Nelson Street in Red Hook, Brooklyn with a towel, a cup and a book. I would lock the door and spread the towel atop the clothes hamper. Then I'd fill water into the cup from the sink and place it and the book on the hamper. I'd hang another towel from my shirt collar to emulate a man of the cloth. Finally, I'd go through the priestly motions I'd seen in church, reciting phrases such as "The Lord is with thee" and imagining the congregation responding.

Far as I knew, my brief boyhood reenactments of priesthood were a closely held secret. No one ever walked in and saw me holding mass. I would've been embarrassed. Also, I'd didn't recall discussing it with anyone and had forgotten about it by my teens. For the purpose of writing this book, I asked my eldest sister, Roseanne, if she knew about my water closet services. She didn't. It's unlikely Tia Montse could've known, either.

It was troubling to have an ambition I'd locked in a psychological vault long ago resurface in such a haunting manner. Could the priest have influenced me as a boy? Did abandoning my desire to join the priesthood convert the cleric into a maniac? Was it possible I entered this world with a spiritual entourage comprised of a wise Jew, a powerful Indian and a priest enraged by my refusal to wear the collar?

I'd always heard we came into this world alone.

CHAPTER THREE

ALMOST HEAVEN

"The career of a sage is of two kinds:
He is either honored by all in the world,
like a flower waving its head, or else he
disappears into the silent forest."

Lao Tzu

After Tia Montse's seance, I returned to work at Paragon Sporting Goods and completed my first semester at Brooklyn College, where I'd taken an interest in anthropology. The professor was a true believer in Darwin's theory of evolution and

29

made a strong case for it using the fossil record. For him, Darwin had disproved the existence of or the need for a Creator. Although I saw merit to evolution theory, I never rejected the idea of a Supreme Being. The finality of atheism was never attractive.

By June 1980, my discontent had ratcheted up. I was turning down the advances of females and was celibate. I recall having conversations about spirituality with a petite, blonde co-worker from Paragon. She was into witchcraft, which I wasn't. During one lunch break in Union Square Park, which was close to Paragon, a group of us sat at a picnic table under which she placed her hand on my thigh. I avoided her after that.

Another time, I tried to get to know a pretty olive skinned Italian woman named Nancy, whom I'd met a few weeks earlier. We had talked briefly on the phone a few times and she finally agreed to meet after work at Prospect Park, where I was coaching a little league team. She arrived at the ball field dressed in a nurse's uniform. We were essentially strangers, having met only once and never so much as held hands. We walked to her car and drove to my basement studio. As I went to the kitchen area to see what was in the fridge, I noticed her standing near the bed. She had already removed her top and was about to take off her bra.

"Oh, hold on," I said, rushing over to look her in the eye. "Don't you think we ought to get to know each other a little bit first?" She looked at me cooly, put on her blouse, grabbed her purse and left. Never heard from Nancy again.

Meanwhile, my old buddies were smoking pot and drinking, but I wasn't. Even though I never tried to convince any of them to quit, my presence caused discomfort. I was lonely, but stubborn. My isolation was inadvertently captured by a photo in the college yearbook. The black and white photo was meant to show the beautiful quadrangle of the so-called *Poor Man's Harvard.* But about midway and to the left, the camera caught me leaning against a large tree, a messenger bag hanging from my shoulder. The sadness of that image, at least for me, was tangible.

At the time, I was struggling to know who I was, feeling phony when I presented myself differently to different people in different circumstances. I literally felt fragmented. I acted one way at work, another way with friends, yet another way at school or another in the presence of a woman. But who was I, really? I believed it could help to spend a week with myself in the mountains. So, I got permission from my boss at Paragon to take the week off and packed the camping gear I'd collected from my years as a Boy Scout. I loved the outdoors and had camped and hiked the Catskills often.

I headed for Grand Central Terminal, but missed the train I'd hoped to catch. I bought a ticket for the next train headed up the Hudson River Line to Poughkeepsie and set my backpack down in the middle of the bustling terminal. I stood behind my backpack in what is known in martial arts as a horse stance, allowing my mind to be in silent awareness.

A tiny Asian woman with a round face and piercing little eyes appeared at my side. Her name was Miyako and I could tell by her accent and name she was native to Japan. She spoke slowly and thoughtfully. We ended up having a nice hour-long chat about life, ideals and spirituality. We exchanged phone numbers and I boarded the train for Poughkeepsie.

Reaching Poughkeepsie about an hour before dusk, I stepped onto the Mid-Hudson Bridge. Part way across, I heard what sounded like two flutes. The way they interacted was beautiful, happy, celebratory. The audible equivalent of two butterflies dancing. First I looked all around to find the source. The radio of a passing car? Nope. I watched cars appear, then vanish from sight, but the volume of the flutes remained steady. Could it be the breeze blowing through the grommets of my floppy fishing hat? I removed it, but the ebullient music continued. Perhaps the wind was whistling through the bridge's suspension cables? Nope. The mild Spring breeze came and went several times during my 3,000 foot trek over the Hudson, but the flutes were unaffected. The source of the joyful sounds remained beyond my reach, but the lightness they brought was more than welcome. I filed this episode away with other unexplained phenomena like the premonitions, waking paralysis and spiritual presences.

The sun was sinking into the horizon as I reached the New Paltz side of the bridge, leaving a chill in its wake. I contacted Joann, who was attending college in New Paltz, from a pay phone to see if she could put me up for the night. I walked and hitchhiked until I reached her home, which she shared with her new boyfriend and others. In the morning, Joann, her beau and I went for a drive looking for a place to drop me off. I sat alone in the rear seat watching as they playfully interacted with one another. I felt and could almost see them locked inside a fragile bubble, oblivious to the world in their newfound love. I was glad to be outside that bubble, having been lost in it with her before.

The couple released me into an unfamiliar wooded area. I hiked up a hill to an open, sunlit field and began walking across it. Suddenly, I felt someone or something watching me. The vibe was bad. I retreated back into the woods for cover until I no longer felt the creepiness. Eventually, I came to a level, clear spot and set up my tent. No sooner than I lie down for a nap, I could hear the panting and running footfalls of large animals closing in. I feared it could be a bear, but it was two large hunting dogs. One barked as they sniffed around the outside of the tent. I remained silent inside. Soon as they left, I packed up. Even though I'd seen no signs, I wasn't sure if I was on private property.

I tried retracing my route back to the road, but soon I realized I was lost and again felt someone or something watching. It seemed I kept going over the same ground - repeatedly reaching a familiar tiny stream with the same contours. The woods grew cooler and I worried I'd be lost in an unfamiliar section of the forest with no campsite and something creepy hounding me. Persistence paid off, and I finally reached the roadway which was brighter and warmer than the woods. With daylight to spare and the creepiness gone, I hitchhiked in the direction of one of my favorite public haunts, Lake Minnewaska.

At some point a compact car stopped to give me a ride. Three people were in it. As was my practice, I memorized their names: Matthew, Judy and Orlando. Matthew, the driver, was a tall, thin man who wore a smile the entire ride. Judy was an attractive brunette with sympathetic, large blue eyes who was seated next to Matthew in the front passenger seat. Matthew and Judy appeared to be hippies in their forties. Orlando, in the back seat, was a friendly young Hispanic American. He helped me get the backpack into the car before we drove off.

Questions followed. I explained how I intended to commune with nature for a week. They were headed to a sleep away camp further north in Accord, New York. Eventually, I saw a good spot coming up and asked if they could let me out. We said our farewells and they watched me walk off into the woods.

The time alone was uneventful, except for a moment when a raccoon and I stared each other down. There was an odd exchange of energy, a light passing back and forth between our eyes. The exchange left each of us satisfied the other was no threat and we both turned and went about our business. This went into my growing *unexplained file*. I set up my tent once again. It was a peaceful night.

In the woods, a fresh insight emerged regarding how romantic relations had caused me emotional pain. Observing Joann and her boyfriend, then being alone with my thoughts, it became clear how the initial thrill of romance had repeatedly been followed by despair. The cycle went like this: through our actions and words we unwittingly created images of ourselves in the minds of the other. The trouble was these experience-based images are false, incomplete, mere stand-ins for ourselves. They have no existence outside of our minds. We sustain these memory-based images by investing emotional energy in them. We cultivate them, adding or subtracting good or bad experiences as we see fit.

We use these images to interact. It's almost like communicating through sock puppets or ventriloquist dummies. We lose direct contact with each other. The images go on to combine and create an alternative world of our own. Encapsulated in a bubble, cut off from the world, we eventually grow bored, alienated and lonely.

That insight was both liberating and challenging. How could I interact without images? Could I see everything and everyone as if I'd never experienced them before, to see the world with an innocent, vulnerable mind? This was fresh on my mind the day I returned to Brooklyn smelling of campfire. I was finally enjoying a long, hot shower when Joe P. announced I had a phone call.

"It's some woman named Miyako," he said.

"I'll call her back," I shouted, refusing to interrupt one of the great advances of modern civilization. "Get her number."

When I returned her call, Miyako asked whether I could meet her that evening to attend a lecture. I agreed and rode the RR train from the Prospect Avenue station into *the city* as we Brooklynites called Manhattan. The address was 4 West 43rd Street, the former Columbia University Club. Miyako and I had just shook hands outside the building when I saw familiar faces getting out of a double parked car.

"Hi Matthew," I called out. "Hi Judy!"

A moment of light-hearted chaos ensued. For their part, Matthew and Judy had recently left me on a desolate stretch of road in the Catskills. How was it I turned up again in their lives so soon. Miyako was puzzled how I knew two other members of the same organization. They each belonged to the Unification Church. My journey from New York City to the mountains and back had been bookended by members of the same religious group. The way I saw it, my introduction to the church was predestined and I needed to pay close attention.

The lecture that evening was interesting and didn't contradict my philosophical leanings.

I agreed to attend a week long seminar in the mountains - at the same place Matthew, Judy and Orlando were headed when they picked me up. Indeed, had I stayed in the car with them, I'd have ended up at Camp New Hope, an idyllic old camp with a small lake and stream located in Accord. For three weeks, I attended workshops, sang songs, ate PBJs and other comfort foods. I met idealistic young people from many states and other nations.

Judy led many of the groups and I met another Krishnamurti alum named Edric. We shared our stories of how we came to be there. He and I collaborated on a song and a female member with a background in ballet performed a modern dance to it. Sometimes attendees were asked to share their testimony before everyone at the camp. When I told my story of searching for meaning, the flutes on the bridge, being alone in the forest and the serendipitous meeting of Miyako, Matthew and Judy, some people found inspiration. Others later confessed they believed I was a paid shill.

It didn't rain for three straight weeks while I was at Camp New Hope. I enjoyed the camaraderie and the lectures explaining the Divine Principle, Rev. Sun Myung Moon's contribution to theology. A quick summary: God created the world to enjoy a relationship with humanity. However, as explained in Genesis, the first humans became alienated from the Creator, who then set about a plan to restore the relationship. That plan involved the creation of Judaism, the anointing of prophets and centuries of sacrifice that paved the way for the advent of Jesus, the second Adam. Jesus was to complete God's plan of establishing a God-centered family on Earth. However, he was murdered before establishing the Holy Family and passed the task on to Rev. Moon during a visitation. Moon, the third Adam, was to create a God centered family to benefit all humanity.

I had no qualms about the church interpretation of history or the notion we needed to live selflessly to restore the world. I felt optimistic about the chances God was real and of life having an original purpose. However, because of Krishnamurti's influence and my aversion to authority, I had trouble accepting the intercession by Jesus, Rev. Moon or anyone else. I remained agnostic, but felt a sense of destiny. In any event, Camp New Hope is where I became a so-called *Moonie*, leading a sacrificial, monastic life for the next six years. Having already renounced many of the physical comforts the world offered and being eager to live an unselfish life, it was an easy transition.

I sold off or gave away nearly everything I owned. The list included several tickets to see Billy Joel at Madison Square Garden on June 26, 1980, an art deco bedroom set I'd restored by hand, and a vinyl record collection. I kept some clothing and a vintage alto saxophone my mother had bought from a local pawn shop upon my graduation from junior high school. My days were spent praying for mankind, sleeping on floors in a sleeping bag, singing songs and *witnessing*, which meant introducing myself to strangers on the streets of Manhattan and convincing them to attend a lecture.

My new affiliation upset family, friends and even some in the Kung Fu school. My mother wept reading a letter I sent her, thanking her for her support over the years and describing my newfound mission. Joe P. and others plotted a rescue. A Sikh who was a Kung Fu instructor accosted me when I visited the martial arts school saying if Rev. Moon was a perfect man he wouldn't defecate.

Rejection and the word *cult* seemed to be everywhere I turned outside of the church. None of this mattered. Persecution was a badge of honor. I was glad to face my destiny with an open heart and mind. Plus I was in the company of great people.

I had no idea I was only weeks away from meeting my Maker.

CHAPTER FOUR

OUTSIDE THE SPHERE

"The Lord is my shepherd; I shall not want. He makes me to lie down in green pastures; He leads me beside the still waters. He restores my soul."

Psalm 23 (NKJV)

After several weeks at Camp New Hope, some of us went for more in-depth seminars at the Unification Theological Seminary in Barrytown, New York. Located on the east side of the Hudson River in upstate Red Hook, the seminary was spectacular. The former Christian Brothers campus, built by John D. Rockefeller, had the air of American aristocracy with stone faced buildings, tiled hallways and expansive grounds with views and access to the mighty Hudson.

It was a warm Summer day. Attendees were encouraged to take time alone between lectures to pray and reflect on what was presented. It was during such a break I wandered toward the Hudson in search of inspiration. However, as I peered down from the lawn to the tidal area below, I was saddened to see a large truck tire and other commercial and residential debris tangled up in the marsh. Some of it had been there for quite some time, partly buried in silt and vegetation.

I climbed down intent on dragging garbage up onto the flat grassy field above. I started with the truck tire. Removing it was strenuous. It was heavy with about a third of it buried in the thick, wet silt. When I tried to lift it and walk, my sneakers came off my feet, remaining behind in the mud. By the time I got the tire up on the grass, I was sweating, dirty and breathing heavily. I set my sights on smaller items after that, tossing them one at a time up onto the grass.

Suddenly, it was there. An overwhelming presence, bubbling and effervescent. It was silent and invisible, but undeniable. It's light, tingling joy filled the air in every direction and consumed me as well. The Earth responded. Every blade of grass, ray of sunlight or whisper of wind produced wonder and ecstasy. Everything was instantly invigorated by a sensitive, loving intelligence. It was untouchable, uncontainable yet more real than any living thing I had ever experienced. This boundless Entity knew everything about me and was overwhelmed with joy to be known by me. It was as if this amazing Being had longed for, waited for and prepared for this moment over aeons.

There was no point where this Entity started or ended. I could not say it was standing over there or it came from that direction. It was everywhere at once. The communication taking place was instant, complete and silent. No words, no symbols or sounds. Yet any misunderstanding was impossible. This was a communion, not a conversation. Whatever message was being conveyed wasn't transmitted in clunky thoughts or ideas. It was direct and efficient. I saw without seeing, heard without listening, understood without thinking.

Being so close, there was no place for confusion to occupy. No way to hide anything. I was totally vulnerable, fully exposed. The Truth was here, alive, sharing itself and asking for nothing. In an instant, the Creator relieved me of all doubt, agnosticism, inward poverty, guilt and pessimism. I knew who

I was and knew my place in the universe: it was all mine.

Standing in the tidal silt, I scanned the skies, the trees, the river off in the distance as they nourished me with a love I'd never known. There was no barrier between the Source of Joy, the creation and myself. The universe was transformed into an instrument of love; love for me, for all people and all things. The sky and clouds, stars and planets, trees and squirrels, rivers and sailboats - all of it - a living love poem to each of us from the Origin of Life.

If I were to put words to the encounter, it would be these: I am here, I have always been here and I will always be here. You are completely known to me and I love you completely. I treasure this moment with you. This is Heaven on Earth and it belongs to you. Go forward in your life knowing there is nothing to fear.

The moment faded and I was once again alone. I didn't return to normal. I couldn't. God was real and life had meaning, value and purpose. Yet now, the Earth, with its Maker once again hidden, was dull like an uninhabited home, an empty chair or an unlit lamp. Beautiful, yes, but incomplete. The blue planet was like a bride who lost her groom on their wedding day. The world was as it was before, only now it felt as if the lights were out.

Perhaps the Communion lasted a second or a minute or an hour. I didn't know and it didn't matter. There remained only the sacred vow of love from an omniscient Creator and my newfound place under the Sun. Sweaty, smeared with dirt, my sneakers covered in mud and without a penny in my pockets, I felt like the richest person on Earth. God planted a treasure in my chest and I wanted to share it with everyone. I had no idea how.

I rolled the truck tire back to the seminar building. Outside the impeccably kept edifice, I asked the first person I met where I could put the clearly out-of-place tire, and for help hauling the rest of the debris I'd piled up on the river bank. A couple of people volunteered and I walked them to the trash site. Two residents of the seminary joined us with a pick up truck, the muddy truck tire inside the cargo bed. We tossed the rest of the junk in. The seminarians drove off to a dumpster. I washed up, changed clothes and returned to the seminar, telling no one what had transpired by the river. That was the day all my thoughts became prayers.

CHAPTER FIVE

DISTILLING THE SPIRIT

"He who is rooted in oneness realizes that I am in every being; wherever he goes, he remains in me."

Bhagavad Gita

O ne benefit of hindsight is being able to put life's experiences in context. The Encounter on the banks of the Hudson River needs contextualization. Divine Visitations have been a part of human experience from the dawn of civilization. They have shaped our world view, established our values and defined us. So let's take a brief look at a few reports of Divine encounters from others to gain a deeper understanding.

According to Old Testament reports, the first encounter with Deity comes when the Creator availed Himself to Adam and Eve - the first humans. Here God is a benevolent spirit who graciously bestowed the Earth and everything on it to the first couple. The means of communication are unknown as neither Adam nor Eve left a detailed account of this idyllic state. Instead, we get this creation story much later from Abraham, considered the author of Genesis. Abraham's account has God speaking in words.

Old Testament prophets like Abraham were a strange and select few who were often respected yet sometimes feared, reviled or even killed. Prophets had wild dreams that predicted future events. Some reported Yahweh speaking in audible words, spelling out specific courses of action for the Jewish people. One prophet claimed to actually see G-d, describing a male with a long, white beard who sat upon a throne of fire. In some Visitations, the Creator appeared in non-human form such as a burning bush, a rushing wind or a dove descending from Heaven.

These Biblical encounters portrayed a once happy G-d who sometimes turned cruel, vengeful or jealous. The prophets sometimes revealed Him as petty, but powerful enough to lay waste to entire cities, inflict plagues and flood the Earth to cleanse it from sin. For righteous believers, on the other hand, miracles happened. Seas parted and food dropped from the heavens. The Abrahamic G-d required strict obedience from His people. Rules governed everything from clothing to diet to personal conduct. The result: a carrot and stick Deity. There are an estimated 15 million Jews in the world today.

The carrot and stick also holds true for Allah, God of the Quran. It is said the prophet Muhammad was visited by the angel Gabriel around 610 AD in a cave three miles from Mecca. The result of these interactions was a codified religion: Islam. Like Judaism, Islam set up a relationship between humans and their Source that is distant, indirect. Humans are tainted by the *original sin* of Adam and Eve and therefore incapable of direct contact with their Maker. In these Abrahamic religions, strict rules must be followed and a clerical class interprets the words of the Supreme and often acts as a bridge between Creator and creatures. There are an estimated 1.9 billion Muslims worldwide today.

Jesus brought a different understanding. Although he didn't explicitly describe visitations by the Almighty, the Bible contains Deific visits to several people surrounding Jesus such as his aunt, Elizabeth and her son, John the Baptist. During Jesus's ministry, Presence was revealed through miracles such as raising the dead, walking on water, healing the sick and restoring sight to the blind.

Jesus's teachings portray a strong, familial connection to the Sublime. He shockingly claimed a father-son relationship with God, which was unheard of at the time. The Prince of Peace illustrated this relationship with the famous allegory of the prodigal son. In it, Jesus described God as a father who is constantly looking for the return of his wayward son, who weeps with joy as he sees his child approaching in the distance and who holds a jubilant celebration upon his return. For Jesus, God is so deeply involved in our lives as to know the number of hairs on each person's head. Jesus also insisted God loved every soul, good or bad and demonstrated this through forgiveness. It is reasonable to believe Jesus directly experienced the Divine just as he demonstrated.

Jesus's new vision challenged orthodoxy. His claim to Divine sonship was considered blasphemous and led to his death. The religion formed after Jesus's death has had a major impact on civilization. However, it also suffered from the same flaw as nearly every ideology: too many adherents believing only their way is right. Christianity goes a step further, citing scripture to assert we can only connect to our Heavenly Father through Jesus. There are an estimated 2.9 billion Christians around the globe today.

In eastern mysticism, encounter with the Source of Life is impersonal, objective, distant. According to Lao Tzu, founder of Taoism:

"There was something undifferentiated and yet complete, which existed before Heaven and Earth. Soundless and formless, it depends on nothing and does not change. It operates everywhere and is free from danger. It may be considered the mother of the universe. I do not know its name; I call it Tao."

Taoism takes a democratic approach to Deity. Anyone who can empty their mind can fill it with the nameless, unknowable presence. Emotional detachment to all things is recommended and the Tao seems to have no personal interest in anyone. There are an estimated 12 million Taoists on the planet today.

Siddhartha Gautama of Nepal, India was visited by an evil demon at the age of 35 while meditating under a Bodhi tree. After overcoming the evil

Mara, Siddhartha received "enlightenment" or an understanding of all things. The means of transmission of this insight is shrouded in mystery.

Siddhartha was initially reluctant to share his enlightenment, thinking it could not be verbally communicated. However, Brahma, the king of Hindu gods, appeared and convinced him to teach. Siddhartha, now dubbed the *Buddha* (one who is awakened), codified his insights into a teaching meant to end human suffering. Similar to Taoism, detachment and a silent mind are stressed. There are an estimated 535 million Buddhists in the world today.

Krishnamurti, who rejected all organized religion, underwent a transformative experience involving a *presence* while meditating under a Pepper tree in Ojai, California in 1922. He later went on to describe encounters with an "immense presence" or benevolent "otherness" in his 1975 work, *Krishnamurti's Notebook*. Here's an excerpt:

"...we went along a narrow one-way street, quiet, with not too many cars; there in that dimly lit street, with few unfashionable shops, suddenly and most unexpectedly, that otherness came with such intense tenderness and beauty that one's body and brain became motionless. For some days now, it had not made its immense presence felt; it was there vaguely, in the distance, a whisper, but there the immense was manifesting itself, sharply and with waiting patience. Thought and speech were gone and there was a peculiar joy and clarity. It followed along the long, narrow street till the roar of traffic and the overcrowded pavement swallowed us all. It was a benediction that was beyond all image and thoughts."

K would later describe his relationship to the "otherness" as impersonal and distant. K didn't seek to approach it or investigate it. He never described it as having its own identity or personality. He suggested there was a "curtain" between himself and the presence and it was not for him to peek behind it. He stressed the need for people to free their minds from conditioning in order to find Truth.

Despite his tremendous insight into the human condition and his mystic experiences, K proved all too human. For example, he carried on an adulterous affair for decades with a close associate's wife. He also condescendingly claimed to be for humanity what Thomas Edison was to the light bulb, stating he did all the hard work and all the rest of us needed to do was "flip a switch." K died in 1986 having refused to establish a religion. The number of people influenced by his teachings is not known. However, as of 2010, more than four million copies of his books had been sold worldwide.

The Reverend Sun Myung Moon claimed he was visited in 1954 by Jesus, who revealed the ultimate Truth in the form of the Divine Principle. Rev. Moon's doctrine, coming from the Abrahamic and Christian traditions, espouses how to reconnect with the Creator through sacrifice. It also asserted the need for intercession between humans and God. Rev. Moon claimed Koreans were God's chosen people and their language was God's own.

Rev. Moon died in 2012, ironically leaving behind a divided Unification Church with feuding factions led by his wife and one of his sons. Like Krishnamurti, Rev. Moon is alleged to have had not one, but several adulterous affairs. The exact membership of the Unification Church is not known, with estimates ranging from 100,000 to several million.

In 1996, Neale Donald Walsch claimed to have a dialogue with The Creator in his best-selling book, *Conversations with God*. At first blush, it appeared the means of Divine contact was a form of *automatic* or *spirit writing*. Automatic writing occurs when a person writes, but the inspiration and material comes from either a spiritual source or from one's own subconscious.

"Abruptly, the pen began moving on its own," Walsch explained in the first chapter of *Book One* of the three book series. "I had no idea what I was about to write, but an idea seemed to be coming, so I decided to flow with it."

Spirit writing has a long and controversial history. Early accounts date back at least to the Song Dynasty in China (960-1279) and continue to this day. Skeptics and researchers of automatic writing dismiss any need for spiritual involvement, finding a person's subconscious mind can account for the phenomena.

However, in written correspondence and a phone interview for this book, Walsch insisted automatic writing played no part in the process that filled his books.

"I would call it 'inspired writing,' and have done so in many interviews,'" he noted. "Inspired writing and automatic writing do not feel to me to be at all the same thing, and do not carry the same connotation or nuance."

Inspired writing involves accessing the Divine voice within oneself, Walsch explained. An experience from my agnostic days helped me relate to what Walsch described. Sitting in silence on a park bench one day, the calm advice "allow yourself to be at peace" entered my consciousness. The phrasing indicated the inaudible words were not mine, nor were they my thoughts. Some other entity was pointing out it was *I* who impeded my inner peace. I found the counsel helpful but never identified the source.

Walsch elaborated on that first encounter with omniscience in subsequent interviews, adding he was startled by an audible voice that came from over his right shoulder. This important detail was not contained in his book. Walsch explained he was initially unsure he had heard a voice but was convinced after recounting the experience with a confidante.

"I now think of what happened at the outset as a purely mechanical response to my desire to not forget exactly what I felt I had heard," he wrote in response to my queries. "From there I found myself engaged in an on-paper dialogue, with the voice I had heard then having moved inside my head."

In 2009, A California woman accused him of plagiarizing her inspirational Christmas story as his own, both in public speaking engagements and in an online post. Walsch claimed he had mistakenly internalized the other writer's experience - an innocent case of false memory. Walsch apologized for the literary trespass, telling the *New York Times* he was "chagrined and astonished that my mind could play such a trick on me." (See *Christmas*

Essay Was Not His, Author Admits, New York Times, January 6, 2009).

Millions have found the *Conversations with God* series, as well as Walsch's other books and seminars, helpful. I read with sincere interest all three *Conversations with God* books. The Deity portrayed in these books is kind, rational, patient and rejects the concept of original sin. More than ten million copies of the *Conversation with God* series have been sold and the first book spent more 139 weeks on the *New York Times* bestseller list.

As you can see, reports of Divine Encounters vary: disembodied words, men on thrones, a loving father, an impartial universal energy, a mysterious benevolence behind a curtain, inspired dialogue put on paper. Sometimes in place of God, the ethereal visitor is an angel or Jesus. What's important is the encounters engendered their own values and worldview. Entire religious doctrines and rituals have been organized around alleged run-ins with Divinity.

Depending on the encounter, believers can be convinced it's impossible to experience our Source directly, or if we can, it will be limited to an impersonal, omnipresent energy. Many people will follow a set of rules and rituals hoping the Alpha and Omega will one day show up. Some could conclude the only way to meet our Maker is to die.

Where does the encounter I attempted to put into words in the previous chapter fit among the recorded visitations cited above? Let's examine.

The encounter I shared is similar to Genesis in that the Makers' presence transformed the Earth into a Garden of Eden, an eternal paradise which was mine to enjoy and share with the world. There was familiarity between Creator and creature. In that way, it also mirrored the vision Jesus conveyed as no detail of my life could escape the unfathomable intelligence.

The Presence was different from Buddhist, Taoist or Krishnamurti encounters in that it had an identity, a thinking, feeling mind of its own. It was fully aware of my being and was actively communicating. Although almost electric in the way it lit up everything with joy, this was no impersonal field of energy.

Unlike the Abrahamic encounters, the Divine didn't speak audibly or take human or inhuman form. Instead, it was silent and invisible with a direct means of communicating that rendered sounds, words and symbols obsolete, a heart-to-heart process I refer to as *communion*.

During our exchange, there was no sense of God being male or female. Likewise, no pre-conditions were imposed on our relationship. I didn't have to adhere to a special diet, go to a church, believe anything or bow to any intermediary. In other words, there was nothing I could do to make the Great Spirit love me any more or any less.

And like the otherness of K, the Divine Presence conveyed innocence, beauty, timelessness and benevolence.

My experience was also unlike visitations from an angel or Jesus, as the Presence had no distinct, identifiable form or location. It was everywhere at once. Somehow formless, but unmistakable.

There may be millions who have experienced Eternal Presence, but chose to keep silent. We'll probably never know. It's not a popular topic to bring up at a party, at work or even in a church, temple or mosque. I know my reaction to someone saying, "I met God" would be skepticism at best. I might even think that person needs professional help. Yet here I am writing a book about it. So why would a rational person risk bringing derision, envy, isolation or loss of career upon themselves? What could possibly be the upside for them? There may be wisdom in silence. I guess we shall see.

That said, I am glad some had the courage to report Divine Visitations which we can explore. There's no sense in advocating for one type of visitation or another. Who is to say audible words or a burning bush is better than a vision? Who will declare some encounters real or some fraudulent? It could be that the Creator found it necessary to manifest differently at various points in human evolution. The message may have changed over time as well. Or perhaps encounters were filtered through the prism of the experiencer's beliefs. But by definition, the Almighty can use any means to reach us.

What's certain is alleged encounters with Deity engendered influential belief systems. Adherents of these beliefs are often at odds with one another. The important question is how the purported encounters with Deity have defined us and shaped our lives. Are we hopeless sinners in need of redemption, the hapless products of original sin? Are we here to obey commandments or risk damnation? Are we beings wracked with inner pain whose only balm is connecting to an impersonal field of energy? Are we incapable or unworthy of communing with our Maker?

And what of those chosen messengers? Time has allowed us to see the humanity of some of them, which I point out not to diminish them nor their contributions to the world, but to discourage putting anyone on a pedestal. We need not be perfect to commune with Divinity. A great musician can make an imperfect instrument sound beautiful.

Finally, I seek not to convince anyone that any Divine encounters ever took place. It is not necessary to accept visitations from the Divine as true to see how these alleged encounters have shaped billions of lives. My aim is to distill context and meaning from a small sample of recorded visitations, including my own, and to encourage others to investigate further. Why accept another's epiphanies when you can have your own?

CHAPTER SIX

GOD RETURNS

"Your pain is the breaking of the shell that encloses your understanding."
Kahlil Gibran, The Prophet

The Summer of 1980 ended and I returned to Brooklyn College in September a different person. The lonely, wandering searcher sporting a mop of wavy brown hair and dressed in jeans and t-shirts was replaced by a confident, well-groomed, driven young man often dressed in suits.

A few other young church members and I moved into a beautiful two-bedroom apartment walking distance to the campus. It was on the sixth floor and featured a large sunken living room with a view overlooking a great expanse of Brooklyn. Our mission was to help people discover God and to establish a chapter of the church's newly-formed Collegiate Association for the Research of Principles, or CARP.

It was an exciting and busy time. We enrolled in classes, witnessed, fundraised door-to-door and on the streets. We prayed often and held seminars in the apartment. We also participated in church holidays. I believe it was January 1, 1981 while attending what the church called "God's Day," that the Presence returned, but in a vastly different setting.

I recall being in the New Yorker Hotel, which the church had bought in 1976. The forty-one story hotel on 34th Street and Eighth Avenue in Manhattan served as church offices, living quarters and a gathering space for holidays. Having studied architecture at Brooklyn Technical High School, I loved walking through the revolving doors into the tremendous, carpeted lobby, taking in the Art Deco design and the huge chandeliers. Church holidays were happy occasions where members from all over the nation could catch up with each other.

Simple food and non-alcoholic beverages were served. Towards evening, we got word to move to a large room where a musical performance by one of the church's rock bands was about to begin. Members began filling the cushioned, interlocking chairs – the kind you'd expect at a hotel conference. I don't recall who was seated next to me, only that we were several rows back from the front and not near either aisle. The lights went low and the band began playing its original songs, which always bore a religious message. I was in a happy mood and it seemed everyone else was, too. Then came a song entitled, *Prisoner of the Heart*.

In an instant the Presence was there, a perfect, scintillating love. It caught me by surprise, seeming to have descended from above and behind me. It was so close. The Presence brought a magical, suspenseful quality and a heightened awareness of all that was taking place in that crowded room. My mind was receptive, vulnerable and calm.

The ebullience was like the prior Visitation at the seminary. However, there were significant differences in the surroundings that were influencing this Communion. The encounter at Barrytown happened outdoors and I was alone. Nature had responded to the glorious Presence, which seemed to bring jubilation everywhere at once. This time I was surrounded by people in a Manhattan hotel with a loud band playing. The Presence almost felt as if it was closer, surrounding me and whispering secrets.

I scanned the room, expecting everyone to be struck by the profound Presence, just as the natural world had come alive during the previous encounter. But everyone I saw seemed unfazed, engrossed in the music. Members sitting mere inches away were oblivious to what I was experiencing. How could they not be feeling this? I looked into the sea of faces around me, hoping to find anyone who was aware of the magic. Just one knowing glance, a nod of the head or smile. But I found none.

The song continued, as did the wordless Communion. Translated from the mystical language of heart, the Holy Presence conveyed something like this: "My beautiful one, I am the source of love and joy. You are the living vessel my bliss seeks to fill. It is nothing for me to pull a star from a galaxy for you. Here, now, know my limitless love for you. Life is meant to be full like this every moment. Now, behold my children."

I again surveyed the room. In this hyper-sensitive state, I felt invisible barriers around each person in that room, which God either could not or would not penetrate. The barriers reminded me of the same kind of insular bubble I had recently sensed around Joann and her beau. Everyone seemed to come equipped with their own invisible force field. That didn't stop the Source of Joy, which hung over all of us in that room, from raining down ecstasy. The unrelenting beauty kept pouring out. But no one felt a drop.

The force fields created limited environments for each occupant, which presented another hindrance to the immense Presence. Our small spheres left no spare room for the Infinite to dwell. So there were two issues preventing Communion - an intangible barrier and the limited space it created.

Blissful Communion continued as the singers repeated the refrain, "prisoner of the heart." It struck me this Precious Being could no more stop loving us than the Earth could stop spinning. Yet, the intended recipients could not be reached. I was witnessing tragic and unnecessary spiritual poverty, the saddest thing I'd ever experienced.

My heart burst with sorrow. "I'm so sorry, Father," I said, my body evidencing my regret by trembling, shuddering and pouring out so many tears that mucous began running from my nose. "I'm so sorry."

As I wept alone in that crowded room, Communion began to fade. My tears subsided. The musical performance ended. There was applause and I was thankful the amplified music and dim lighting had covered my weeping. The lights came back on and I kept my head down as people began leaving. I wiped my face the best I could and walked out of the room, avoiding conversation with anyone. I found a restroom, where I blew my nose and washed my face. I'm not sure how that evening ended, but most likely with a subway ride back to Brooklyn, a place the Dutch settlers named *the broken land*.

CHAPTER SEVEN

PIERCING THE SPHERE

"Your task is not to seek for love, but merely to seek and find all the barriers within yourself that you have built against it."

— Jalal al-Din Rumi

O ver the years, I've gone over and over the second Visitation searching for an understanding that could be the solution to my spiritual alienation. The initial takeaways were mixed. I felt sure we could all live with inner abundance if we stopped walling ourselves off. But I also came to the sad realization Divine Visitation was something I had no control over and could not pass along. I tried sharing parts of the Visitations with family and a few close friends over the years, but no Divine encounters resulted for them.

This dilemma and the writing of this book forced me to reexamine spiritual alienation from Source. I brought my mind back to that evening in the New Yorker hotel to explore the moments just before I began weeping at the sight of people who were unaware of the immense Presence in that room. The first thing that came to mind was the absence of guilt or blame for our alienation from God as suggested by the concept of original sin. My fellow church members were innocently unaware of God's Presence. They were not intentionally blocking out bliss. I searched through the exchange that took place during communion and found no accusation or anger or frustration coming from the Divine Presence. I detected no sense God was repulsed by some kind of stain or irrevocable sin. There was only love and longing.

So what, then, keeps us apart? There clearly is an invisible barrier between each of us and the world, each other and God. The innocence of my fellow audience members brought to mind a fitting analogy: that of a fetus developing in the amniotic sac. It is alive, but not fully experiencing life. It can think and hear and feel, but it cannot walk the Earth or enjoy the fullness of physical life. It is nourished, but cannot yet enjoy a cooked meal. It is inside it's mother, and so unable to feel her embrace or touch her face. It can move, but not dance.

Similarly, we see with our eyes, but not always with our soul. We hear perfectly, but do not always listen. Our state of spiritual alienation seems to be a result of the intangible *sphere* that delineates where *I* end and everything else begins. This elusive barrier may serve legitimate functions, as does the amniotic sac. It could be protecting our immature spirit as it develops until it is ready for the next leg of the journey. Like a fetus, it could prove fatal to be ejected into the world too soon. Conversely, it might also be dangerous to remain in the womb too long.

Perhaps at this stage in our evolution many of us are floating inside a spiritual womb, alive, but not yet *born* into the fullness of communion with our Source. We can see a tree, yet not be moved by it. The direct connection to the outside world is blocked until we shed our spiritual orbs. Once outside our protective spheres, a tree is no longer just a tree, but a source of nourishment, joy and wonder. Born into Reality, we understand the word "tree" is not the actual tree. The mental image we hold of a tree is not an actual, living tree. Yet, for most of us, the image holds sway over the reality. Once beyond the sphere we are no longer confined to interacting almost exclusively with our memories, thoughts and dreams. We are capable of direct contact with the world.

Direct contact is possible and soul nourishing. I recall one morning just before sunrise when the song of a bird entered the Brooklyn apartment I shared with other church members through an open window. Outside the window an indigo sky blanketed the morning with silence. Brooklyn was asleep and dreaming. Suddenly the bird's song shattered the stillness with a sound so rich it penetrated to my core, sending waves of joy through my mind and body. The episode reminded me of a story about a preacher who stood before his congregation about to open his mouth when a songbird landed on the window sill and interrupted. "The morning sermon is over," the minister said.

Getting back to what closes us off from such encounters, let's continue our exploration of the spiritual enclosure I refer to as *the sphere* using the amniotic sac as our analogy. This is not some wild new theory. There is Biblical support for this view. For example, Jesus mentioned we needed to be "born again" during a late night conversation with a Pharisee named Nicodemus. "Most assuredly, I say to you, unless one is born of water and the Spirit, he cannot enter the kingdom of God. That which is born of the flesh is flesh, and that which is born of the Spirit is spirit. John 3:5-6 (NKJV)

Jesus' disciples repeatedly described how he intended to help humanity experience life more abundantly. When questioned by Roman authorities regarding his claim to be a king, Jesus pointed out his kingdom was a spiritual one. In his famous prayer Jesus seeks God's kingdom to be established "on earth as it is in heaven."

I think it safe to say Jesus alluded to our being spiritual embryos on our way to being born into a more abundant state of existence. Similarly, the Visitations I've attempted to describe revealed a more abundant life is available on Earth but requires us to emerge from the protective sacs we unknowingly inhabit. The means of *being born* again for most Christians requires one to profess and accept Jesus as our saviour. While this may save souls from eternal damnation, it does not bring us into direct Communion with God or the creation. It doesn't end our spiritual alienation here on Earth.

We may be embryonic spirits awaiting birth into a more abundant life. We develop in our ethereal wombs, dreaming, knowing vaguely there is more for us *out there*. But wombs are, presumably, safe, warm and comfortable places. Don't babies cry in protest when forced to leave?

The necessary discomfort of birth reminds me of the suggestion Jesus offered a wealthy young man: "If you want to be perfect, go, sell what you have and give to the poor, and you will have treasure in heaven; and come, follow Me." Matthew 19:21 (NKJV) Jesus went even further, rejecting his physical family in favor of his spiritual kin.

Taken figuratively, Jesus's teaching is similar to Eastern mystics who claimed enlightenment comes to those willing to psychologically "die" to the past, to all they've achieved and accumulated - even their loved ones.

This is not a call to live in amnesia, loneliness or poverty, but to inwardly let go of attachment to things, people, memories, fantasies. It is a call to approach life with an innocent, beginner's mind which holds no preconceived notions or prejudices. It is a call to see things as they are right now - and not through the prism of experience and the past. It may seem painful, even counter-intuitive at first, but the rewards are immeasurable.

What proof is there the spheres we inhabit really exist? You cannot see, touch, smell, taste or hear the invisible borders. However, we can verify the existence of our boundaries simply by looking into what we call our *personal space*. Here's an experiment anyone can try: while sitting across a table from someone, take something of yours - a beverage, a tissue, a book - and place it more than halfway across the table near the other person. You should feel two things: your entering the other person's *space* and their discomfort. If that doesn't work, just grab their beverage before they take a sip and drink some. The border you will have crossed is neither physical nor visible. But it's real enough to know you've violated it.

Our spheres are flexible. They can grow to include other people, material possessions and ideas. All the things which define *who we are* fill our spherical environment. The existence of isolating spheres are further confirmed by language we use daily such as of *me, my, mine, I, ours*. We refer to a workplace as *my job*, we sit at *my desk*, and so on. At home we have *my wife, my children* and *my bed*. Our invisible boundaries are physically expressed by the fences and security devices we put around our homes, businesses, vehicles, money.

Borders are nothing if they aren't enforced. Now we are touching an entirely different topic: the origins of violence. Intrude on the personal space of some people and you can provoke a violent reaction. An intrusion could be verbal, such as questioning someone's belief or challenging their assessment of themselves. It could be physical, such as standing too close or chatting up someone else's paramour or spouse. Much of our law centers on invisible boundaries and the rights and responsibilities they involve. Many wars have been fought over trespassing of some sort.

A world of heartfelt connection, free of violence, starts with each of us becoming aware of the barriers which enclose us, separating us from everything else. Awareness requires a beginner's mind, one in which there are no goals or motives. We simply observe without judging what we encounter as either good or bad. We allow ideas, memories and impulses to present themselves and naturally fade. The quality of attention itself will dissolve the sphere.

Once again, everything presented here is a mere suggestion for your further exploration on your own. No one can do this for you.

CHAPTER EIGHT

CONTROVERSY AND SYNCHRONICITY

"His sorrow was not solitude, it was that other gulls refused to believe the glory of flight that awaited them; they refused to open their eyes and see."
                              Jonathan Livingston Seagull
                              by Richard Bach

Controversy marked my years at Brooklyn College and in the church. At school, persecution and acceptance was the norm. *Moonies* were feared and despised on campus, especially by other religious groups. Despite repeated attempts to establish a C.A.R.P. chapter at B.C., following all the rules, the student government repeatedly rejected our applications. This went on for five years. At one point, the New York Civil Liberties Union got involved, seeing a civil rights violation. In the end, I wasn't allowed to officially organize the chapter.

Academically, I opted for a dual major of Philosophy and Journalism. Philosophy, I hoped, would sharpen my reasoning skills and explore what the greatest minds had to say on epistemology, ethics and the existence of God. I was disappointed Krishnamurti was not on any course menu. However, by the time I took a debate class, I was unstoppable. The course required competing with another student in two debates. Myself and another student each took a side for or against a proposal to build the contentious Westway highway project in Manhattan. The issues involved were environmental, traffic, costs and so on. Classmates judged the presentations. A few weeks later, we switched sides. I won both.

Journalism, I figured, would help me communicate more effectively. My journalism mentor, Tony Mancini, encouraged all his students to write for the school paper of record, *The Kingsman*.

At *The Kingsman*, I started out at the bottom and went on to run the news and feature sections. Miraculously, by my final year I was elected Editor-in-Chief and my re-election vote was unanimous. The BC administration was terrified I'd brainwashed the entire *Kingsman* staff and would turn the paper into a Unification Church propaganda sheet. It was nonsense but there was nothing they could do to reverse the elections.

Back at the church, things weren't going too well. Despite my best efforts, not only wasn't I able to establish a C.A.R.P. chapter on campus, I couldn't bring in any new members. Students would attend lectures, but not the longer workshops designed to enroll members. I was replaced several times as leader of the center. It was humiliating. However, my spiritual life was active.

For example, I recall once falling asleep in an armchair while studying only to awaken paralyzed. I struggled to move, but couldn't. Then, for the first and only time in my life, I called out for Jesus to help. Suddenly I was filled with love and sensed a bright Presence standing in front of me. I fought to open my eyes, but couldn't. My arms and hands were still locked in place, but I felt the warmest love down to my fingertips. I was then able to open my eyes and get up from the chair. I saw no one else in the room.

Other spiritual experiences included repeatedly feeling as if there were flames coming from the left side of my chest. It was so real one time, while standing by a door in a subway car, I started swatting flames that didn't exist. When confronted with unexplained phenomena like this, I would sometimes pray and open the Bible to a random page. I opened to Isaiah 48:10: "Behold, I have refined you, but not as silver; I have tested you in the furnace of affliction." (NKJV) Several times my heels felt they were aflame. The random Bible page for that was Romans 16:20: "And the God of peace will crush Satan under your feet shortly." (NKJV)

In October 1982, I was married in a mass Unification Church wedding of some 6,000 couples in Korea. Several months earlier, I had my lone interaction with Rev. Moon in the Grand Ballroom of the New Yorker Hotel. Members sat on the floor, men on one side and women on the other. Rev. Moon, who spoke almost no English, casually paced up and down the aisle that separated the sexes. An interpreter asked questions about members' education and other criteria. A handful would be picked and asked to stand. Then Rev. Moon would match couples. We didn't choose our spouses because we had to live unselfishly to repair our strained relations with the Almighty.

When it came my time to be matched, he looked me over and spoke in Korean to his interpreter. The interpreter asked whether "father" had previously matched me to someone. I said "No" and was then paired with a slightly older Japanese woman. She spoke almost no English, but Miyako served as our translator. The only question my future bride asked was whether I had any sexually transmitted diseases. Americans were under-appreciated in the church. The marriage was never consummated and later annulled. Also around this time Rev. Moon founded the *Washington Times* and I was chosen to be part of it. However, Miyako set up a meeting with another respected member who convinced me to complete my studies first.

Nineteen Eighty Two was also the year I met my biological father. My mother had run into a friend of my father's while shopping. A meeting was arranged in her backyard. He looked like a bigger, older version of myself. He gave us a summary of his life: a boxer, a Navy SeaBee during World War II, a barkeep and now a maintenance man at St. Vincent de Paul Society in downtown Brooklyn.

The relationship was cordial, but strained. On one hand, I was confronted with the pain I'd buried from childhood as it emerged from the shadows.

The many times I ended questioning by telling others my father "died in the war." The time I caught a glimpse of the big man in the t-shirt and black-rimmed glasses from the backseat of a moving car. "That's your father,' some adult in the car said, pointing. Then there was the time when I was about sixteen and my mother thought I really needed to spend time with my father. She tracked down his parents and we knocked on their door, but they pretended to know nothing.

Over the years, I had a recurring dream of being chased. During one such dream, I stopped running and turned around to confront whoever had been chasing me. It was my father. We looked at each other and he just shrugged. On the other hand, his love of swing music and Frank Sinatra led me to pick up the saxophone again.

We met many times over the years until he passed away in 2007. I believe being raised without a father animated me to pursue answers to life's basic questions. Is there a God? Does life have a higher purpose? Fatherlessness also drove me to seek guidance in the form of religious teachings and philosophy. Perhaps the void left in my psyche by my father's absence was an opportunity for the Creator to step in. I do not know. I do believe God arranged the meeting with my father so I could confront the pain created by his abandonment and take a step towards wholeness.

My father's appearance raised an intriguing question: could my incomplete identity - resulting from his absence - have something to do with the Visitations? In other words, was I more vulnerable or accessible to the Presence because I didn't have a strong sense of self? A little research revealed several historical figures who claimed to encounter God, Jesus or angelic beings had lost or been separated from one or both parents.

Moses had been abandoned in the Nile River shortly after birth by his mother. From the Biblical account, it's unclear who Jesus's biological father was. Buddha's mother, Maya, died seven days after his birth. Muhammad lost his mother at the age of six. Krishnamurti's mother died when he was ten and he was separated from his father shortly after. There is little early biographical information on many of the Old Testament prophets, and what is available is often incomplete or unreliable.

Synchronicity has always been a common thread. For example, a friend told me in April 1983 she might have a spare ticket to see Krishnamurti at the Felt Forum. If this ticket wasn't claimed that evening, I could have it. I was surprised to hear K was coming to New York because I had sent him a letter in 1978, naively inviting him to stay in my apartment if he came to the Big Apple. I received a reply from his secretary bluntly stating K would never set foot in NYC again, but I was free to make a monetary donation. In any event, I got a call at the last minute: the ticket was available. I attended the talk with three or four others, who all fell asleep. I was glad to finally see my mentor after being led to believe it would never happen, but most of what he said I'd already internalized.

In hindsight, I now see the Divine working to address deficiencies caused by life without a father. There was shame and a feeling of inferiority at school, where I spent my days with well-off kids in the city's Intellectually Gifted Children program. Their fathers were doctors and lawyers. They wore ironed shirts and pants. Their shoes were polished. I wore thrift store shoes and clothes and had a birth certificate with the father's information section left blank. I recall building my first bicycle from a frame and parts I found at the Department of Sanitation dump on Hamilton Avenue, just off the Gowanus Canal. I never owned a GI Joe like my friends. If it was popular and advertised on television, I didn't have it or expect to get it. So, during this period of life, I felt God lifting my chin, letting me know the days of want and shame were behind me.

I graduated from BC in 1985 and took a reporting job at the Unification Church owned *New York City Tribune*, where I covered an array of topics including politics and crime. Loved reporting and got my first taste of breaking a big story when I received an invitation to donate money to pay for "porta potties" that were to line an upcoming Gay Pride parade. The solicitation said the toilets would have names added to them to mock various conservative figures. For example, one was to be named the "John Cardinal O'Connor Throne Room" to ridicule the prominent Catholic leader.

The story had legs. The portable toilet company announced they wouldn't be renting their stalls to be used to bash public figures. That put the entire parade in jeopardy because portable johns were required in order to obtain a parade permit. I also discovered the fundraiser was run by an assistant commissioner for the city's Department of Corrections.

The tempest in a pee pot story was picked up by other newspapers, on radio and television and led to an official corruption investigation. A news clipping of it later helped secure a job at the *New York Post*.

Tribune employees had to cash their checks at a nearby bank. On February 16, 1986, I stood in line at the bank and I saw a man several spots ahead of me reading the *New York Times*. I was pretty sure I saw Krishnamurti's photo in the paper. When I returned to the *Tribune*, I flipped through the *Times* and found K's obituary.

By 1986, I was again struggling. Covering crime deeply disturbed me. There was the "Spiderman Rapist," who clambered up fire escapes and through apartment windows before tying up men and raping their wives or girlfriends in front of them; or the Mariel Boat Lift madman who savaged riders on the Staten Island Ferry with a machete. I struggled to fathom why people would act in these ways.

At the same time, I was uncomfortable every time my editors asked me to participate in church activities. In retrospect, even though I was twenty-six, I was still psychologically vulnerable. So I left the news business with no other prospects in sight and no official affiliation with the church.

A friend suggested I become an educator, so I took a job teaching inner city school kids. That ordeal with the New York City Board of Education lasted seven years. The bright spot in this period was meeting my wife, Deorajie (her English nickname is Kathy) in 1989. My Golden Retriever ran ahead of me one morning and jumped on Kathy as she headed to work. Comet's large paws rested on her shoulders and his nose was inches from hers. She was petrified. So was I: Comet was supposed to be on a leash. I ran over telling her not to worry, that Comet wouldn't bite and commanding my loyal buddy to get down. Holding Comet by the collar, I apologized to the most beautiful woman I'd ever met. Thick, wavy black hair framed the sharp features of her face - large pecan brown eyes with long, natural lashes and perfect eyebrows, an aquiline nose over full lips that eventually opened to an innocent, brilliant smile.

Kathy and I had lived on the same street for more than a year, but our different work schedules had prevented us from meeting. She had been running late the day Comet introduced us. It would be weeks before we'd see each other again, but when we did, we took time to chat. Soon we were meeting for a few minutes each day after work. At some point, her family entered the picture.

Kathy is of East Indian descent, which presented formidable obstacles. First, she was the youngest child and all of her married elder siblings had taken part in traditional arranged marriages. She was already matched to someone from her own culture when we met, although she hadn't dated that person or seen him for a few years because he wasn't in the United States. We met the kind of resistance from family you might expect when long-held traditions, racial, language and cultural barriers are challenged. We pressed on.

Kathy invited me to the apartment she shared with her family, where her mother would ply me with roti, curry and tea. Her father had little to say to me. At one point, he came up with a surefire plan to get rid of me. He had found a combination lock at work and passed it around to his colleagues to see if they could open it. Satisfied that no one could, he then passed it among family members with the same result. Finally, the day came when he emerged from the living room and showed the lock to Kathy as we sat alone at the kitchen table. He told her I would have to open the lock if I wanted to marry her. Then he put it in her hands and walked back to the living room.

With a distressed look, Kathy gave me the lock. It was one of those padlocks with three small wheels at the bottom that could rotate and stop at any number from zero to nine. Locks like this have 1,000 possible combinations. I methodically started turning the wheels. To my surprise, it popped open after just a few combinations.

"Here you go," I told Kathy, smiling and placing the opened lock in her hands. "Give this to your father." Kathy got up and headed to the living room while I remained at the kitchen table, smiling. Silence.

The rest is history. We married and bought a home. Kathy finished college and became a

Registered Nurse. Our family grew to include our firstborn, a son.

By the Summer of 1993, I felt teaching in the city public schools was too toxic and was seeking a change. One evening, my former journalism professor, Tony Mancini, called my home. "Would you be interested in working at the *New York Post*?" Mancini asked.

"Where do I sign?" I replied.

The *Post* was in turmoil at the time, but I was eventually hired in August. The next month I was fired because the writer's union declared a strike. In October, I was called back. My eleven year tenure at the Post was remarkable. I cultivated loyal sources in the FBI, DEA, NYPD, US Marshals, judges, prosecutors, civil and criminal defense lawyers, Hollywood - you name it. With their help, I earned a reputation as a fierce competitor who broke several exclusive stories per week. I was sought out for television commentary about crime, the Mafia and terrorism, and was twice nominated for the Pulitzer Prize for investigative reporting.

Through it all, I spoke to my Maker constantly. My thoughts continued to be prayers and the answers came through synchronicity or through music.

CHAPTER NINE

FAITH TESTED

"First they ignore you, then they laugh at you, then they fight you, then you win."
Mahatma Gandhi

From 1993 until today, several major events took place which I attributed to God's ongoing involvement in my life. The pattern was this: a severe struggle followed by an amazing turn of events.

In 1993, I was a NYC public school teacher working at a tough junior high on the outskirts of Park Slope, Brooklyn. The principal wanted to get rid of me for what he considered offenses. For example, once I called the school security officer to my room so he could secure a knife found inside a desk. Juan and I had become friends after he heard me playing the sax before school started. He wanted to learn music and he came to my house several times for lessons.

But Juan told me he was mistreated by the principal, who didn't want him to file any reports of violence or security threats to his bosses at the Board of Education. If Juan felt strongly enough about an incident, he would have to use the payphone outside the building. The principal grilled me about my reporting incidents directly to Juan and began a brutal campaign to make my life miserable.

I have always made a poor victim. So one year I got permission to start a school newspaper. A handful of students were picked to be reporters and I began teaching them the art of journalism. We set up a mock press conference with the principal. The students needed help with questions to ask. I provided topics, including school security. The press conference ended abruptly.

While the administration worked to get rid of me, many teachers quietly supported me, enough to be elected to a newly formed school based management team. The team shared power with the administration on all policies. Well, efforts to get rid of me got more intense and the teacher's union ultimately reached a deal in which I agreed to leave with a satisfactory rating at the end of the school year.

Kathy was pregnant with our son, Jiddu, who was named after Krishnamurti. We had just secured a mortgage for a two family brick row-house in the Kensington section of Brooklyn. And I was out of work. About two months into my wife's pregnancy, she slipped coming down the stairs from her parent's apartment. I was in the kitchen and ran to her and we discovered she was bleeding from her vagina.

We immediately called her doctor. After a physical inspection and X-rays, the doctor said some internal damage had been done to the placenta that was causing the bleeding and our best option was an abortion. I asked what other options we had and she said my wife could try lying in bed with her legs raised for the duration of the pregnancy. There were risks the fetus could die inside her and, if that happened, Kathy's life would be endangered. The doctor set up an appointment for an abortion at the hospital.

Kathy and I discussed the devastating news on the drive home. We had looked forward to our son's birth, having seen sonogram images of him in the womb and preparing for his arrival. Each visit to the doctor had revealed another milestone in his development and filled us with more anticipation. Kathy was swallowed up, unable to make a decision whether to try to save her baby or take the doctor's advice. We spoke with family members. Everyone agreed we should get the abortion. Kathy was not able to envision it. The choice was left on my shoulders. I prayed for guidance. There wasn't much time.

"Let's cancel the procedure," I finally said, sending shockwaves through both sides of the family. Everyone believed I was putting Kathy's life at risk. I withstood enormous pressure, yet feeling God's assurance of a good outcome. We began making preparations for Kathy to remain in bed for the next several months. That included her not returning to work and coordinating her care with her mom, dad and sister on my work days.

Soon the bleeding stopped. Kathy was able to get up and walk around. Doctor visits resumed. On the day Jiddu was born, I was in the delivery room. The moment he emerged, I felt a joyful tingling my chest that immediately brought the Visitations to mind. It felt as if God touched my heart with one finger as if to say, "See. We did it."

Jiddu brought great joy to the family. He grew up to be a caring, intelligent young man who is now in his third year of medical school.

The new school year was approaching, and I dreaded having to go back to teaching. I had no job lined up. One evening, Tony Mancini called and soon I was working at the *New York Post*, where my career soon hit overdrive. Some editors dubbed me *Ally Wood*, the "wood" being the term used to describe front page stories. I won't delve too deeply into the stories as there were hundreds of exclusives over the years. Suffice it to say I would find myself in the right place at the right time or cultivate a source who would end up in the perfect spot to feed important stories. People would read my stories and contact me with even better ones. Eventually, I developed sources in federal law enforcement and earned a reputation for coverage of the Mafia and terrorism.

Synchronicity was key to my success. Here's one example. On the tragic 9/11 terrorist attack, I remained at home in Brooklyn because travel into Manhattan was nearly impossible and cell phones didn't work. My landline at home did. The *Post* routed a call from an agent of the D.I.A (Defense

Intelligence Agency). The agent asked about a series of stories I wrote about two months earlier in which the INS and the FBI had questioned and released three Middle Eastern men who had drawn suspicion for the photographs they took of landmarks and federal buildings in Lower Manhattan.

The feds confiscated the film and let the suspects go, determining there was no reason to detain them further. But when the film was developed, all hell broke loose: the photos were focused on security apparatus at several federal buildings.

"Is there anything else you recall about this," the DIA agent asked.

"I'm sorry, but everything I know about that is in the stories," I told the agent, whose name I am withholding. I promised to call if anything further developed.

Two days later, I got a call from an officer from a state agency who was working the massive rescue and recovery mission at the Twin Towers site. He had gone into a building volunteers were using to wash up at the end of their shifts when he passed a cubicle belonging to the U.S. Marshals Service. Pinned to the wall was my story about the release of the three men the feds had let go. Stapled to the clipping was a bulletin containing the names and photos of the men, along with other information on why they were being sought. I met the state officer at a diner in Staten Island at 2 am.

The photos and the two page spread in the September 16, 2001 edition of the *New York Post* about the feds' search for three alleged terrorists they had released in June sent shockwaves through the federal government, New York City, Washington, D.C. and beyond. The night before it was published, I called the DIA agent to let him know what to expect.

"You're an American hero," he said at the end of the call. The stories ended up being part of Congressional inquiries into the lack of inter-agency coordination in the fight against terrorism. That led to greater cooperation between federal and local law enforcement in terrorism matters. I believe the DIA may have used the story to help justify moving terrorism into the military realm and, in some areas, push out law enforcement.

In 2001, I was nominated for my second Pulitzer, but not for that story. It was for another that led to increased protection against terrorism of the New York City water supply.

Meanwhile, the principal who made so many teachers miserable, was keenly aware his staff now had a sympathetic ear at the sixth largest newspaper in the nation. I recall someone mailing me a copy of the teacher's union newspaper with a photo of the principal on the cover under the headline, "The Principal From Hell." I had nothing to do with it, but I admit laughing.

At the *Post*, I got to know and meet people from all walks of life. From Presidents and Counts to the criminally insane and serial killers. I appeared on numerous television shows and documentaries, most of them about the Mafia. My phone was always busy and I cannot say how many invitations I received or how many people sought my time. I'm not a name dropper, but I will offer one example: In May 1996, the actress Bo Derek from the movie *Ten* called my home several times after I broke a story about her being named in a lawsuit by Time Warner over a film contract.

The film initially called for Bo to ride naked on a horse along the seashore in a pay-per-view movie. But Warnervision executives added scenes of rape and other sex acts that portrayed her as a raging nymphomaniac, prompting her to reject the changes. The film company sued for breach of contract. Bo and I never met, but she expressed her gratitude after Warnervision dropped the suit and quit the movie business altogether.

By September 2004, the editors who valued my presence at the paper were gone. I knew my days were numbered at the *Post* not long after an expose I penned that involved the purchase of a lion cub. It's a long story involving actress and animal rights activist, Tippi Hedren. Bottom line, it helped draw attention to a problem, a federal law was passed and all ended well. But my editors weren't happy with the controversy the expose stirred as the paper was ridiculed for weeks by its rival, the *New York Daily News*. The "Snooze" as we called it, got the story completely wrong and never corrected it.

I felt the bullseye on my back. Just before the axe fell at the Post, I was working on a piece about illegal firearms in the city with one resource being Dan Rather, Jr., a Manhattan prosecutor I'd gotten to know over the years while working on gun trafficking stories. I called Dan Jr. to let him know I wouldn't be completing the project. He mentioned he was going fishing upstate New York with his famous father and that he would bring my situation up. I thanked him, but doubted anything would come of it. My last story for the paper ran on Sunday, September 19, 2004.

After eleven amazing years I was summoned into an office and fired for reasons that were never really clear to me. The plan was to have security immediately escort me out to the street, but a well respected senior management official stepped in.

"You can't do that to him," she protested. "There's no need for security. I'll take care of it." The editors backed down. I cleaned out my desk as she worked on the terms of my departure. She then walked me out.

So, there I was out of work again with Kathy pregnant again, this time carrying our daughter, Almitra. I kept busy updating our partially finished basement. On Monday, September 27, 2004, at 3:15 pm, my cell phone rang and I heard a strange but familiar voice on the other end. He was jovial and sounded as if he knew me.

"Who's this," I asked.

"I'm sorry," he chuckled. "This is Dan Rather." I now recognized the voice and instinctively looked for a television set.

We set up a meeting in his office at the CBS building on West 57th Street. We shook hands and I handed him my resume and a binder filled with newspaper clippings.

"Your reputation precedes you," Mr. Rather smiled and said. "You are a tomb of silence."

We had several meetings. Mr. Rather introduced me to executives at Sixty Minutes, Sixty Minutes Two, the CBS News network and WCBS local. At a meeting with the local station, they went through clippings I'd compiled in a binder. They wanted the station to be more competitive and break more stories, but they challenged my lack of television production experience.

"Why should we hire you?" one executive asked bluntly.

"Don't hire me," I replied. "Let me break some stories for you and you pay me only for what airs."

They agreed. Within six weeks of my submitting invoices for what aired, they put me on staff. I learned how to produce investigative news segments for air, which was more cumbersome than print. I broke some stories about 9/11 and other topics. I worked with the FBI on a terrorism related story that included an underwater interview in Lake Minnewaska with a member of the bureau's scuba team.

After two years, I was ready to move on. I found the television news business shallow and my old school, gumshoe journalism not appreciated. I took the next opportunity that turned up: buying a hotel and restaurant in the Catskills.

It was a leap of faith for Kathy and I, but we sold our Brooklyn home, left our jobs and jumped right into the hospitality business. We purchased the Catskill Mountain Lodge in 2007. We raised our children in the country and spent lots of time together running the Lodge. The kids developed advanced social skills working in the hotel and restaurant. I took care of maintenance and managed the hotel and restaurant. I was also able to improve my saxophone chops and perform with world class Jazz musicians in the venue I created in our restaurant. Kathy was a warm host who was loved by guests, many of whom have become friends. She also handled employee scheduling and payroll. The Lodge allowed our little family to learn and grow together.

At this point in my journey, I'm able to reflect on how I blossomed from a lonely, troubled, fatherless boy into a man leading a full life. Through every challenge and every victory, I saw the hand of my Creator. There's no such thing as serendipity.

CHAPTER TEN

CULTIVATING CONNECTEDNESS

"Yesterday I was clever, so I wanted to change the world. Today I am wise, so I am changing myself."

Jalal al-Din Rum

A t this point, you may wonder, is the experience of Divine Visitation open to anyone? What can I do to have my own direct encounters with God?

There is no reason to doubt each of us has the capacity to experience God's Presence directly because we all possess awareness and consciousness. But just how sensitive are our minds to things going on around us? To what extent do we feel the presence of one another? Do we feel connected or do we often feel alienated?

There's no need to sit in the Lotus position or recite a mantra to discover how connected or alienated we are. You don't need guided visualization. You can find alienation anytime, anywhere and it costs nothing. Look around. Watch the people you pass on the street or in an Internet cafe, how they may not even acknowledge your presence. The person walking around with their faces glued to a cell phone. Notice how some never make eye contact. See how they are locked in their own little worlds.

Now ask yourself what you feel emanating from them while in their presence. Are they happy or sad? Are they lonely or troubled? What impressions do you pick up? Optimism? Open mindedness? Kindness? Or just the opposite? Or maybe you feel nothing. This should not be surprising at this stage of our spiritual development.

If you aren't sensitive to the presence of those you can see, how do you expect to feel the Presence of something invisible?

Jesus noticed this and put it this way: "If a man says, I love God, and hates his brother, he is a liar: for he that loves not his brother whom he has seen, how can he love God whom he has not seen?" 1 John 4:20 (NKJV). Therefore, developing a more sensitive awareness of the people and things around us is a good place to start.

Awareness can be dulled or heightened by life experience. For many of us, the field of our awareness grows smaller over time. Think of the mind as a camera. The aperture is the part of a camera that opens and closes to adjust the amount of light that gets in. Our minds adjust this way. For example, when we see a beautiful or wealthy person our aperture may widen. We become very interested in that person and begin to take in all sorts of information about them. The reverse is also true. We see someone who appears to have nothing to offer and the aperture closes. Our awareness of them shrivels.

An extreme example of this is the stereotypical middle management employee of a business who flatters those immediately above them on the corporate ladder but ignores or abuses those below. They know all the details of their bosses' lives: their likes and dislikes, the names of their children and pets, their life stories. They remember their birthdays, are always supportive and laugh at any attempt at humor. But they invest little or no energy getting to know those they consider beneath them.

Most of us are unaware of the widening and narrowing of our awareness or its implications. One result is many of us walk around walled off, living in a state of alienation from much of the world around us. In extreme examples of alienation, people become dead inside. They're called sociopaths. They are unable to empathize with others. Thankfully, they are outnumbered.

The good news is our fields of awareness can be expanded. We can observe the aperture process as it takes place. We can feel the biases we've developed closing us off. We can also feel the swell of interest we have for specific people or things. Most importantly, we are also capable of a motiveless attention which may enable us to step outside our intangible speres. Like a flame, our innate intelligence can burn through the mist which clouds our days. There's plenty of material available on the topic of expanding awareness (see the suggested reading section).

Let's examine the impact limiting awareness can have on spirituality. The world of spirit is subtle and to perceive it the mind must be sensitive and open. On the other hand, walling ourselves off can leave us in a state of spiritual alienation. This inner emptiness is akin to grief. We intuitively know something is missing. There is a longing inside us that won't quit.

Like material poverty, spiritual poverty can cause desperation, even addiction to things, activities and people. It is a curse to be dead inside, to feel nothing while looking out at a sunrise, to be unmoved by the lighted path moonlight creates on the water or the laughter of a child soaring on a swing. Inward desolation leads us to impulsively pursue sources of gross, often self-destructive stimulation. We intuitively know we are supposed to feel elated, full, happy. Inner spaces meant to sustain the flower of perfect joy are overtaken by weeds of self-centeredness, guilt, shame and inner conflict. How many people have we met who are desperate for attention? Needy? Self-destructive? Soul draining vortexes of drama? No one can fill the void in such a person.

Our educational systems do not prepare us for this. Hardly anyone talks about it. To dull the pain, some fall prey to unhealthy beliefs about themselves, the world and God. Hucksters and drug dealers will take your money and offer you temporary relief. Relationships, even if they are destructive, can become a temporary escape. Mind altering drugs, both legal and illicit, wreak havoc on millions of lives. Hollywood makes handsome profits taking us on brief trips to fantasy land. The media? Have you ever heard the phrase "spiritual poverty" during a newscast?

Religion, for the most part, distracts us from our alienation from Deity with tales of great miracles past and sacred rituals. Robes, incense, relics and prayers help to cover God's absence, albeit briefly. At best, most belief systems encourage us to have faith God will enrich our lives if we believe and pray. We hope to meet our Maker after we die. Meanwhile, we are here now, separated from our spiritual Source and suffering the consequences.

My suggestion is to invest time deepening your awareness of the people and things in your life. Practice trying to sense the presence of someone in the room. Listen to the wind, to what people say and do not say. Look at what is shown, but also at what is hidden. Take a moment to hear - as if for the first time - the moaning whistle of a distant train or the chirping of a bird outside your home. Watch a small bird leap from a tree branch, spread its tiny wings and fly - without the word "bird" getting in the way. Little things are capable of producing limitless joy.

Many make time to hit the gym or do a yoga class, which is good. Others take great pains to eat healthy foods. This is also good. However, we could also make time to care for our inner world, to stretch our minds. This can be done at any time - during the morning shower or commute, while at a meeting or on a date, or over a meal or while at a computer. Weakening the barriers that we've built around ourselves may open up a place at our table for the Source of Life. Dinner will never be the same.

We can make a great contribution to the future by raising our young with an eye toward broadening their awareness. Engage them in activities which do not reinforce barriers or confine them to the contents of their own memories, thoughts and imaginings. For example, it's preferable to raise them with a pet, which has a life and personality of its own, rather than dolls and figurines which have no life other than the one the child imposes. Likewise, would it not be better for children to engage in group activities such as dance, music, sports, outdoor hikes and camping rather than spend hours on video games?

Always encourage children to think of others. For example, a father can ask a child what they have done for their mother that day; encourage them to perform some act of kindness for a family member each day. It could be making a cup of tea for mom or hanging up a bathrobe. Make it a routine to ask what the child did that day for someone else, perhaps at dinner time or before bed. Before long, they will come to understand that thinking of others is something we expect from them. This is not to say they should not care for themselves. No one can properly care for another if they don't care for themselves. The point here is to raise conscious, sensitive children who are capable of balancing their interests with the interests of others.

Parents can also lead by example. For instance, my daughter still recalls the time we were on a family vacation and about to enter a restaurant when we encountered several blind people struggling to find the entrance. No one seemed to notice, not even the employees. So, I walked up to the group and asked one of them to hold onto my arm while the rest held onto one another. Together we carefully walked single file into the cavernous eatery up to the maitre d's station, where I explained the group's situation.

Engaging in meaningful activities with others and having good role models can reduce insular mindsets, leaving our children in a better position to empathize with animals and humans alike. Such a childhood renders an adult who is more sensitive to the vitality within all living things. It puts mental activity within the context of an engaged, creative and empathic lifestyle so it doesn't degrade into self-centeredness and isolation. I humbly suggest we can find many ways to broaden our childrens' sensitivity and awareness, leaving them more open to experiences of Divine Presence. There is no greater gift.

CHAPTER ELEVEN

MAKE THE LION MOVE

"For assuredly, I say to you, whoever says to this mountain, 'Be removed and be cast into the sea,' and does not doubt in his heart, but believes that those things he says will be done, he will have whatever he says."

Mark 11:23 (NKJV)

There's one story I enjoy telling that illustrates the magic of a life of faith. It was the Summer of 2000, Kathy, Jiddu and I were spending many weekends in an old fixer upper we bought in the Catskills. Every time we pulled off the New York State Thruway at Exit 20 we'd see a billboard for the Catskill Game Farm featuring a male lion and the words, *Lion around waiting for you*. One hot Summer day we decided it was finally time to visit the iconic Game Farm.

We drove to the nine hundred acre menagerie to spend the entire day. We rode the railroad and fed goats and other animals. Jiddu, seven years old at the time, rode atop an elephant and we were entertained by bicycle riding bears. We saved the lion exhibit for last.

As we approached the lion section, it was unnerving. There was a low wall, no more than three feet high, over which you could see a male lion and a handful of females lying on the ground one behind the other. From any distance you got the impression these apex predators could easily jump the low wall and attack anyone. Yet several people were calmly gathered at the wall, looking on and chatting as if everything was fine. I'd seen some unusual things in the boondocks, so I told Kathy and Jiddu to wait while I approached the wall. To my relief, there was a steep trench on the other side to prevent the lions from escaping.

I gestured to my wife and son and we stood at the wall watching the lions for a few minutes. The sun was beating down hard and we'd been walking the sprawling property for hours. The lion scene was anticlimactic, albeit true to the billboard ad. The four or five lions just lay there on the right half of the enclosure panting in the sun, tongues hanging. All three of us felt let down.

Two men in Game Farm uniforms were chatting at the wall so I asked, "Do these lions ever move?"

"Nah," one of them replied. "At the end of the day we open a gate back there and they'll walk through that over there," he said, pointing to an opening in the chain-link fence. "We do that when it's feeding time."

"And when is that?" I asked.

He checked his watch. "In about an hour."

I looked at my son. His disappointment showed in his eyes and pouting lips.

"You want to see the lion move?" I asked.

"Yeah," he lightened up.

I never liked preaching. But I saw a chance to demonstrate faith. I took a breath and prayed (by this point, nearly all my thoughts were prayers anyway). I recalled Jesus asking, "What man is there among you who, if his son asks for bread, will give him a stone?" Matthew 7:9 (NKJV) So why wouldn't God grant this wish? All I wanted was to pass my faith on to my son in a concrete way. Besides, what I was about to ask would harm no one.

I faced the listless lions, raised my arms and said, "Lord, make the lion move."

Then we waited. In the hot sun. It seemed like a long time. Nothing. My mind wandered to how a normal person could try to make the lion move by yelling, taunting or tossing something into the enclosure. But that would defeat the purpose of having the Creator move the beast. Instead, I focused on the Love God had promised me. I was certain that having designed that lion, and at that very moment sustaining every molecule in its body, the Creator surely knew what would get him going.

"Let's get out of here," Kathy said, sweat beading on her forehead.

"No. Wait," I protested. "The lion's going to move."

By this time Kathy had known me for about ten years. She'd learned to be patient with me when it came to invoking God. So Kathy sighed and waited.

Then seemingly out of nowhere a chipmunk appeared to the far left of the exhibit. It picked up a Saltine type cracker from the ground. The cracker looked big in its mouth as it looked around in small, quick movements. The male lion stared. His focus intensified. The chipmunk headed for the chain link fence, cracker in mouth. The lion ever so carefully rose up. The chipmunk began poking his head through the small diamond-shaped openings in the chain link, but the cracker didn't fit. The little rodent poked here and there to no avail. Meanwhile, the lion started walking stealthily, then trotting, then running towards the chipmunk, who dropped the cracker and jumped through the fence.

I've shared this story a handful of times. Reactions have been as varied as the people I've told. Some have found encouragement in their faith. Others questioned my motives for telling them. Still others tried to find explanations that do not require faith. For example, one young man explained how I could've pre-planned the entire event in my subconscious.

For my part, I ask this: would you rather live a life of pessimism, stagnation and doubt or one in which the lions move?

CHAPTER TWELVE

MUSIC OF THE SPHERES

*"The artist alone sees spirits. But after
he has told of their appearing to him,
everybody sees them."*
        Johann Wolfgang von Goethe

In the wake of the Visitations, music became
one way to feel God's continued involvement
in my life. After all, it is the "universal language."
Learning about music over the years, I believe

it is the language of the Creator because it can communicate directly with our hearts.

At any time, I could be moved by a song. It could happen anywhere and it could be any song. Pink Floyd, Harry Chapin, Dan Fogelberg, the Moody Blues or Elton John are just a few examples. It is easy for me to believe the Creator inspired the music and lyrics, which cover a range of emotions and ideas. Some songs inspired a joyful response while others produced melancholy, even tears. I'll offer a few examples and excerpted lyrics.

In some songs, I feel God's love, sadness and desire to reach us:

Watching and Waiting by the Moody Blues (1969)

Soon you will see me
'Cause I'll be all around you
But where I come from I can't tell
But don't be alarmed by my fields and my forests
They're here for only you to share
'Cause here there's lot of room for doing
The thing you've always been denied

This song reminds me of God's timeless love for us, as does the next one:

Longer by Dan Fogelberg 1979:

Longer than there've been fishes in the ocean
Higher than any bird ever flew
Longer than there've been stars up in the heavens
I've been in love with you

Stronger than any mountain cathedral
Truer than any tree ever grew
Deeper than any forest primeval
I am in love with you

Blessed by Elton John (1995)

Hey you, you're a child in my head
You haven't walked yet
Your first words have yet to be said
But I swear you'll be blessed
I know you're still just a dream
Your eyes might be green
Or the bluest that I've ever seen
Anyway you'll be blessed

Some songs are more poignant:

Hey You by Pink Floyd (1979)

Hey you out there on your own
Sitting naked by the phone
Would you touch me?
Hey you with you ear against the wall

Waiting for someone to call out
Would you touch me?
Hey you, would you help me to carry the stone?
Open your heart, I'm coming home

This is one of several songs which affirmed some aspect of my spiritual condition:

Taxi by Harry Chapin 1972:

Whoa, I've got something inside me
To drive a princess blind
There's a wild man, wizard
He's hiding in me, illuminating my mind
Oh, I've got something inside me
Not what my life's about
'Cause I've been letting my outside tide me
Over 'till my time runs out

There are many, many songs I could add to this list. Music is but one of a million ways the Great Spirit may be trying to reach us. Movies, books, the people we meet, an unexpected phone call, the wonder sparkling in the eyes of a child. All we need is a receptive mind and heart.

CONCLUSION

"To the mind that is still, the whole universe surrenders."

Lao Tzu

I want to thank you for sharing this journey with me. I hope you've found value in our time together.

Socrates said the unexamined life is not worth living, and I agree. I've enjoyed examining my own life almost as much as I've enjoyed biographies. I've read many: George Washington, Kahlil Gibran, Pablo Picasso, Krishnamurti, Clint Eastwood, Sam Giancana, Mahatma Gandhi. We can learn from one another. Epic victories and tragic defeats are wonderful teachers. I hope sharing my spiritual journey will help someone on theirs.

We've covered much ground. From seances and sleep paralysis to Divine Visitation and the challenges life poses to our faith. Through it all, I've tried to present the facts as clearly and succinctly as possible with respect for the reader. Along the way, I've touched on subjects that could be explored in more depth. After all, this book was not intended to be the final word about anything.

When discussing this project in the early stages, a friend asked whether readers might question why God chooses to commune with one person and not another. Are some people better, superior or more spiritually advanced? My answer is twofold: no, and I don't know. I say "No" because historical accounts show God has conveyed messages through humans who were far from perfect. In addition, I assure you I am a work in progress, physically and spiritually. I'm still searching. For years I've wondered why the Visitations mysteriously started and then stopped. Did I have anything to do with either? Will there be at least one more Meeting before I depart? I don't even have answers to some of my own questions.

What is more difficult to know is how or why God chooses to appear at certain times to certain people. Who can know how a mind capable of designing something so vast and complex as the Cosmos reaches its decisions? I believe it's safe to say our Maker acts to benefit our development, even though that end may not always be clear to us.

Imperfect as I am, one thing drove my writing: I am convinced infinite joy was intended to be the baseline of human existence, our daily experience of the world. Divine encounters are not meant to be reserved for anyone special, nor to be occasional or random. The happiness of Communion belongs to everyone, all the time. The further God's boundless love can reach, the better. Imagine a time when we no longer fear one another or live behind locked doors. I welcome the day poverty and oppression are distant memories. I fully expect inward desolation to be replaced by fullness of heart.

Too many have been led to believe in a distant God - up in the sky or in some far off, inaccessible place surrounded by fences and gates. Is it any wonder we feel alienated from our Source when generations have passed down beliefs that turn out to be obstacles? What if the Creator is surprisingly close? Could it be God dwells in the silent life force pulsating within you, supplying the power to feel, to see, to hear, to taste and to dream? If we must have beliefs, why not consider this: that God bears silent witness to all your days; that together you butter your bread, kiss your children, dance and weep?

Imagine for a moment God is not merely the distant object of your dinner time prayer, but the prayer itself, and the voice that carries it, and the scent of the food and the warm plate and the table it's on. Imagine being enveloped by and inseparable from your Source - the only distance being that which you create or allow.

Today we may be ensconced in our separate orbs, preparing for that dream job or our first home. Perhaps we're making room for a new member of the family or pursuing the girl next door. We could be fretting over that math quiz or wishing we had a puppy. But at some point, we are likely to find ourselves longing for something more: a deeper connection to God, the universe and one another. We have the means to get there. We can look compassionately at ourselves - the happy and sad memories, our beliefs and values, the way we treat and react to one another. With a beginner's mind, we can dissolve the intangible barriers we've inherited or built up over the years.

The process of loving self-reflection is noble and worthwhile. It will render our hearts and minds more vulnerable, innocent and free, enabling us to see ourselves in others and in all things. We will have accomplished the kind of deep, significant and lasting change our world truly needs, not the shallow type promised by politicians or obtained through the force of law. At times this approach may seem thankless and lonely, but take heart. Synchronicities will appear from time to time to uplift you. Perhaps an even more powerful benediction will emerge: the subtle Majesty that awaits each and every one of us just beyond the sphere.

SUGGESTED READING

Below is a partial list of books I recommend to anyone earnestly searching for Truth and direct contact with Ultimate Reality.

1. *The Prophet* by Khalil Gibran
2. *Jonathan Livingston Seagull* by Richard Bach
3. *The Flame of Attention* by J. Krishnamurti
4. *Krishnamurti's Notebook* by J. Krishnamurti
5. *The Tao Te Ching* by Lao Tzu
6. *The Reality of ESP: A Physicist's Proof of Psychic Abilities* by Russell Tang
7. *Hierarchy of Needs: A Theory of Human Motivation* by Abraham Maslow
8. *The Gateless Gate: The Classic Book of Zen Koans* by Koun Yamada
9. *Living, Loving and Learning* by Leo Buscaglia
10. *The Road Less Traveled: A New Psychology of Love, Traditional Values and Spirituality* by M. Scott Peck
11. *Life in the World Unseen* by Anthony Borgia
12. *The Self-Actualizing Cosmos: The Akasha Revolution in Science and Human Consciousness* by Ervin Laslo